every year since 2009, with rising 1
attacks and stress being the leading c....... .. ..

The millions upon millions of prescription drugs being taken worldwide would suggest a species that is not able to cope with life as it is. Then there are the illegal drugs like heroin and cocaine that have been the mainstay for people wanting to experience different states of mind. More recently methamphetamine, or ice as it is known, is becoming the illegal drug of choice. The illegal drug trade is huge, both in money terms and the terrible effects on many lives. Police forces around the world seem incapable of being able to deal with the problems that the trade in drugs is causing.

Many people struggle with moral dilemmas, or wonder what the purpose and meaning of life is. Religion is supposed to fulfil this human need for spiritual guidance, but many activities based on religious beliefs are difficult to understand. For example many religions are at war with each other which openly defies two well known Christian laws of 'Thou shall not kill' and 'Do unto others as you would have them do unto you.'

The Catholic Church has more wealth than a lot of smaller countries, and from my own understanding, if there really was a God, He would be disgusted that so few people have so much, and yet millions of others live in poverty.

Paedophilia is rife within the churches and many are strongly paternalistic in nature.

The various religions are also struggling to come to terms with the proven science of evolution, which explains the creation of life in a much more understandable and scientific way than religious beliefs are able to do.

A solution to the problem

This book explains how the human species evolved within the energy that we call love, and this loving energy has been the main reason for humanity's successful evolution. It has also fulfilled our ethical, moral and spiritual needs. The blocking or repression of this energy in the human brain is causing it to malfunction. If we can get this energy of love flowing again I believe most of the problems of the human race will be resolved in a natural and calm way.

If we want to understand the nature of love, and how a fatal flaw in the evolution of the human brain is denying access to this love, then we need to rethink the activity of the brain from an evolutionary perspective. This is achieved through the three levels of consciousness model that embraces the cortex as the cognitive brain, the limbic system as the feeling brain, and the brainstem as the sensing brain.

Our brains developed upwards from brainstem (sensations) to limbic system (feeling) and then later the cortex (cognition). For a long time during our evolution we were a sensing/feeling organism. Then we developed a cortex and became 'thinkers'. As we developed our new found cortical 'thinking' intelligence, we came to rely on this part of our brain for survival. Our sensing/feeling brain (that relies on the transmission of love between humans to function properly) was pushed into the background.

When a child does not receive love from a parent, it registers this situation as rejection from the family and clan, and therefore life itself. The response in the child includes feeling extreme pain; a pain so powerful that it cannot be felt without danger to the survival of the child. Therefore it is repressed away from conscious awareness. The pathways in the brain that are used to repress emotional or primal pain also block our access to feelings of love.

Nearly fifty years ago Arthur Janov stumbled upon a way to unblock this pathway in the brain and allow the love to flow again. He called the therapy Primal Therapy because dealing with the lower levels of the brain is primal in nature.

In 2004 I went to Los Angeles to undergo this therapy that opens up the pathways between the three levels of consciousness. Accessing the primal pain stored in my brainstem was a difficult and emotionally draining process. The force of the energy locked away was awesome, and I found out these same forces had been the cause of my suicidal depression, social anxiety and addictions.

A positive outcome, which I was not expecting, was that as the pain was felt and released, it opened up the pathways to my loving feelings. Allowing loving feelings to flow through my body, after a lifetime of experiencing mostly negative emotions, was a difficult process within itself. My organism was not used to such feelings, and seemed to treat them as foreign invaders. Now I understand when people talk and write abstractly about spirituality, the soul, the God within, positive aspects of religious doctrine, the Tao or the modalities of self healing, what they are all describing comes from the force of pure love that is generated from brainstem sensations.

About this book

When you read this book you will need to have an open mind because

1.   I write about the three levels of consciousness which are not generally understood within the psychological, psychiatric and other counselling professions, or the lay public for that matter. Love is a function of the sensing/feeling brain and in the hierarchy of power and influence within the three levels the sensing brain is by far the strongest. The fatal flaw exists in the human brain because of the blocked information flow between the three different levels.

2.   I explain how primal therapy works in relation to the three levels of consciousness. There are many versions of primal therapy being practised around the world but I discuss Janovian Primal Therapy because I believe it to be at the cutting edge of understanding how the brain works, and then it uses that knowledge for effective therapy. If you ask anyone from the general public about Primal Therapy they will either not have heard of it or say that it is ineffective and/or dangerous. Janovian Primal Therapy is very effective because it understands the brain in terms of how it developed during its evolution, and so therapy is conducted within these necessarily tight parameters.

In the right hands the therapy is not dangerous.

3.   The notion of love seems to exist as being very esoteric in nature. This book explains how it is a function of the lower brains and is anything but esoteric. It is a very powerful force. I experience it in my body/mind as a sensation or resonance that guides my thinking and actions. The resonance of love in the human body is, I believe, the healing force that keeps us healthy, both mentally and physically.

The key to a happy and meaningful life is to have free-flowing access to our sensations of love. For this to happen we need to understand and overcome the nature of the fatal flaw within the human brain.

4.   This book talks a lot about primal pain, and reading it may trigger your own unresolved pain. Be aware that this may happen, and if your reaction becomes too severe don't hesitate to seek help, either from local mental health professionals or telephone help lines.

5.   This is not an academic style of book in that I have referenced all my statements. I feel I have given enough information that if the reader wants to access the original quote or research article then Google, in this day and age of electronic wizardry, is the place to search.

Robert M. Pirsig in '*Zen and the Art of Motorcycle Maintenance*' had this to say, "*Traditional scientific method has always been at the very best 20-20 hindsight. It's good for seeing where you've been. It's good for testing the truth of what you think you know, but it can't tell you where you ought to go."*

This book is not so much about where researchers have been, as much as trying to explain where they ought to go.

Gilbert Bates
February 2016
Perth, Western Australia.

A FATAL FLAW

A lthough this book is mostly about the nature of love, I will start the discussion by explaining what I believe to be a fatal flaw in the human brain. This fatal flaw denies humans access to their feelings of love. I will try and show how this flaw in the evolutional development of the human brain has already been responsible for millions of human deaths, and if our understanding of this flaw does not change swiftly and radically it will continue to be responsible for millions of more deaths. This fatal flaw is so powerful and so entrenched in the current human psych that it may eventually cause the extinction of the human race.

The psych's (psychologists, psychiatrists and other counsellors) understand the brain as having two areas of psychological significance, these being the prefrontal cortex (PFC) for cognition and the limbic system for emotions. Historically, the cognitive brain has received the most attention, but the so called emotional brain is gaining more focus, probably because of its irrepressible presence. Neuro-scientific techniques are improving and demonstrating that activity in the limbic system can now be measured and related to feelings and emotions.

But the so called emotional brain can be divided into the limbic system and the brainstem. This factor is extremely important in understanding the fatal flaw, because the brainstem sensations are the driving force for the rest of the brain. The current approach to mental illness does not understand the power of the brainstem, and so the prefrontal cortex is deferred to when encouraging a client to override negative thoughts; thoughts that actually arise from a dysfunctional brainstem. Many forms of cognitive behavioural therapy and psychotherapy are based on this concept.

The triune brain model works on the understanding that there are three important areas, or levels, of the brain involved in human experience and perception. The cognitive brain is the top layer and is centred in the prefrontal cortex. This area lies above and behind the eyes and deals in abstract thought and in this book will be referred to as the third level of consciousness.

The second level of consciousness is the limbic system which lies deeper in the brain. Anatomically the limbic system lies roughly between the ears in the centre of the skull, and deals in feelings that create emotions. Note that the psychological profession normally discuss emotions and feelings as the same thing, but they are different. A feeling is generated first and then comes the emotion. We are sad (feeling) and then we cry (emotion), or we are happy (feeling) and then we smile (emotion). We can feel a feeling and no-one else may know what we are feeling, but when we show emotion the people around us know what we are feeling. In terms of understanding mental health the distinction between emotions and feelings is very important.

The third part of the triune brain, and the least understood in psychological terms, is the brainstem. It extends from beneath the limbic system down into the neck area where it joins with the spinal cord. The brainstem deals in sensations; it is known that the brainstem has biological senses that control things like oxygen levels, heart rate and alertness levels, but it is not so well known for its effects on our psychological state. This is the first level of consciousness, the one that is oldest in evolutionary terms. It is also known as the reptilian brain that dates back to around 300 million years ago.

The triune brain consists of three levels of functioning; the cognitive (thinking), limbic (feeling) and brainstem (sensations).It is important to note that thinking, feeling and sensing create three different mind states. Of the three the brainstem sensations are by far the most powerful and largely determine what happens in the other two levels. The way we *sense* our lives influences what we feel and what we think. The brainstem carries the memory of our earliest experiences, including our time in the womb. If we were loved our memories will produce loving sensations, and these generate our feelings and then feelings give rise to loving thoughts and actions. If we were traumatised (not loved) our traumatic memories will reflect that in unloving (neurotic) thinking and behaviour.

How do I know all this?

I had a depressive breakdown at age 46, and my first attempt to fix the problem was to see a psychiatrist. He put me on medication and told me I may have to be on them for the rest of my life. Intuitively I knew that wasn't a cure, and he could not explain to me what was happening inside my head. This was particularly frustrating for me, because I am a man who likes to know how things work.

Exploring alternative therapies led to situations where I was able to cry while feeling excruciating emotional and physical pain at the same time. After these episodes I felt much better and I knew I was seeking in the right direction, so much so that I was able to take myself off medication. I wasn't cured by any means, but at least I could function without the medication.

Eventually I found out about Janovian Primal Therapy (JPT) and it resonated with my previous experience of feeling type therapies. This therapy understands the triune brain system, the absolute power of the memories held in the brainstem, and the power of the brainstem to affect the two levels above it.

The therapy process takes a person, in a gradual way, from his thinking mind and into his feelings (as separate from emotions). From the feelings the exploration continues down into the brainstem where the imprinted painful memories are sensed for what they are. There is no analysis by the therapist, no drugs to take and no manipulation of the thinking process. *Sensing* the past and then releasing the attached pain is all the person needs to do to get better. It is the repression of painful experiences that makes us sick in the first place, both mentally and physically. Releasing the pain by feeling it within the context it was experienced will allow the mind and body to heal by itself providing that we also supply our body with good nutrition!

How is this approach different to the current psychological paradigm?

Primal therapy is a feeling/sensing journey where the person gets to experience their body and mind states as a thinking, feeling and sensing organism. In so many people the feeling and sensing brains are repressed and so they form part of their unconscious state of mind. Primal therapy lifts the repression so that feelings and sensations become an important part of our conscious state. We repress feelings because they are not pleasant, forming a divided brain in which our thinking and feeling brains are not 'talking' to each other. After the unpleasantness is felt, we then become free to feel the love that is generated from this level of human functioning.

The psychologists have cognitive behaviour therapy (CBT) which tries to change thoughts and behaviours by telling the cognitive brain to think and act differently. This works to some degree because we do have some free will over the power of the brainstem. However the person will always have to control their symptoms because once they let go, the brainstem memory that has been imprinted is the default programme. Talking to the brainstem does not work because the brainstem has a sensing function that does not understand speech or ideas. Remember that the three levels provide different ways of experiencing and perceiving the world.

Psychotherapeutic and psychoanalytic approaches do not work because they don't go deep enough into the brain. A psychoanalyst is observing behaviour and speech and trying to analyse what is wrong with the patient from these observations. The psychoanalyst cannot experience what the person is feeling, let alone the underlying sensations that drive the feelings. Analysis of this third level of functioning is mostly useless because it does nothing to alter imprinting at the first level of consciousness in the brainstem.

Psychiatrists rely on medication to reduce the myriad of mental disorders from which the human race suffers. Medication changes brain chemistry in order that signals from the brainstem do not impact heavily on the cognitive brain. In most cases this reduces symptoms of disorders like anxiety and depression, but notice that this treatment does not treat the actual imprints. When the medication is stopped the symptoms will return. Medication in the form of SSRI's not only block painful feelings but they also block any good feelings, thereby reducing the person's ability to feel love and joy. The brain is numbed down.

Now we come to a very important point in understanding human behaviour, which also explains the basis of the fatal flaw. If we have imprinting (see next chapter) of good early life memories at the first level, the sensations generated flow freely into the second level which generates good feelings, and these good feelings flow upward in the brain to the third level, where good thoughts and actions flow from the cognitive brain.

If these early memories (imprints) are traumatic it creates a huge pool of primal pain. When our parents do not love us in the way we need to be loved our very survival is at stake, therefore our memories will carry the force of near death experiences. These forces are important in understanding the strength of the fatal flaw, and are sensed by people who approach near death imprints during primal therapy.

In the infant these terrible experiences are repressed away, because if they came fully to consciousness the cognitive brain would be overwhelmed and become dysfunctional, even to the point of death. We have sad evidence of this in Eastern European orphanages. As late as the twentieth century, despite having all their physical needs met, children in these orphanages were dying in large numbers. In the beginning the carers were not allowed to give the children any attention, such as play, touching or cuddling. But when this order was revoked the death rates dropped dramatically. (Children from these orphanages have been adopted by people in other countries on a large scale, and much research has been conducted into how they develop after their traumatic beginnings).

If we have imprints of 'bad' memories then the feelings produced will also be 'bad'. These bad feelings are overwhelming and must be kept from conscious awareness. To avoid these feelings the brain changes them into what we perceive as being acceptable thoughts and actions. They are neurotic thoughts and actions that form a major part of any persons defence system, the system that keeps primal pain repressed and out of conscious awareness. The psych industry has a book called the Diagnostic and Statistical Manual of Mental Disorders (DSM.V) which lists all the symptoms of a disordered brain, and from this book we are given a diagnosis of narcissist, psychopath, bi-polar, depressed, anxious, and dozens of other human brain disorders. From a primal theory perspective they are all symptoms of a brainstem that is holding onto memories of painful experiences.

Primal theory says depression occurs when the brains defence system has to work extra hard to keep painful feelings repressed and anxiety occurs when the locus ceruleus in the brainstem has registered terror in the early years of life.

How do I know this? Why hasn't current research uncovered these processes? The answer is that research is conducted at the level of the cognitive mind only, or third level of consciousness. Psychology and psychiatry in their current states can be viewed as the 'thinking man's' view of mental health.

Primal therapy is an actual experience of the feeling (second level) and sensation (first level) part of the brain. During therapy a patient is encouraged to reduce their thinking process while being directed toward their feelings. The painful feelings are released in small doses over many sessions and as this process progresses psychological symptoms will reduce, no matter what the official diagnosis is. The narcissist and the psychopath will become more loving and so enjoy their lives more, in addition to being more pleasant for others to be around. In my case the depression and anxiety ceased.

The fatal flaw is based around the fact that overwhelming bad feelings that are rising up through the brain structures are converted to thoughts and actions that can be classed as irrational and/ or neurotic. An extreme example is the paranoid person who sits in a closet with a tin foil hat on his head so that extraterrestrials cannot communicate with him. Underneath all those crazy ideas is the pain of an unloved childhood, which probably contains aspects of not being able to communicate with his parents. One of my own act-outs was to eat ice-cream instead of feeling my need for a hug. Alcohol, cigarettes and illegal drugs are all physical activities that help to reduce painful feelings from coming to conscious awareness. A lot of these activities are harmful to our health and cause many deaths each year.

Now the reader can begin to understand why certain brain processes end up being fatal.

Perhaps the biggest killers of people are the *ideas* and *beliefs* that are generated by a defence system that will do anything to avoid primal pain from coming to consciousness. I am talking about religion and politics in particular and will expand on their effect in later chapters. Strangely enough the current psychological paradigm understands that the brain creates irrational ideas as a means to reduce otherwise disturbing feelings. But they still try to change the symptom (irrational idea on the third level) rather than deal with the cause (the imprint on the first level).

An aspect of the defence system is that it operates at a subconscious level, and so we are not aware that our thoughts and behaviours are governed by the need to repress primal pain. Most of us think that we are very intelligent and rational, and we carry very little primal pain. This is a profound delusion within the brain of the human species. We all have more pain than we can imagine and this pain is the cause of nearly all human suffering. Even though primal patients come to therapy knowing they have to deal with their pain, everyone I know is surprised at the amount they carried and the effect it had on their (mostly miserable) lives.

If primal theory understands most of the causes and consequences of traumatic imprinting then it is prudent to ask why people in high and influential places aren't doing something positive about rectifying the situation. My answer is that all university courses are intellectually based, in the sense that only the cognitive brain is being utilised to try and understand all psychological problems. They do not understand that other parts of the brain are involved, especially the brainstem sensations that exert such a strong force. This force cannot be understood by reading a book, it must be felt for what it is to appreciate its strength and dominance in brain functioning. Until the psychologists are required to experience ten or fifteen primal feelings that involve the brainstem and limbic system, they will not understand the basic mechanisms behind common mental disorders such as depression and anxiety. They may be able to read about it in a book one day (like this one) and come to understand it in a cognitive way, but there is no substitute for actual experience. The difference between thinking something and actually feeling it is quite extreme.

Arthur Janov discovered the primal process nearly fifty years ago, and has successfully treated thousands of people, including myself, by addressing the limbic feelings and the brainstem imprints. He has had trouble trying to explain the process to his peers, mainly because academic learning is very intellectual in nature, and does not include any processes that require students of psychology and psychiatry to feel their feelings and sensations. Janov has been writing books on the subject, but writing and talking are very different ways of communicating knowledge as compared to the knowledge that feelings and sensations communicate. The implicit knowledge contained in sensations and feelings has been more than three hundred million years in the making (Evolution. The Human Story. Dr Alice Roberts) and has been an important part of our successful evolution. The disconnection from this part of our human brain may be the cause of our extinction!

There is one other important thing that happens when a person gets to experience primal pain, and it is the main reason I am writing this book. There is absolutely no doubt in the mind of a person who has undergone primal therapy that the vast majority of psychological disorders are caused by not getting our needs met by our parents. The pain that is generated when we come to finally accept that our parents did not love us in the way we needed is extreme - it is mind-bendingly overwhelming. It can only be felt in little 'chunks' over many sessions. I talk from personal experience and have also witnessed many others going through this painful process. Patients are not expressing ideas and theories about what the causes of depression and anxiety are, and what the cure may be. We have sensed and felt both, so further discussion and theorising is irrelevant. We know the causes and the cure because we have experienced them. It is terribly unfortunate for the rest of the population that we have no way to convey the knowledge that our sensations and feelings have given us.

Not everybody is in a position to undergo primal therapy, but if our species understands the causes of our problems, we can all take steps to create a society that knows how to love its children. Some people respond negatively to this information. However despite the relationship between parent and child being vitally important, that same parent-child relationship needs to occur within a culture that is structured to raise healthy children, and that means everyone is involved. It takes a village to raise a child!

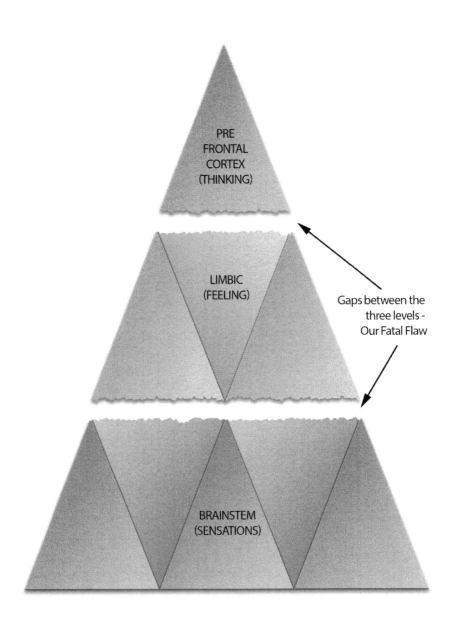

PRE
FRONTAL
CORTEX
(THINKING)

LIMBIC
(FEELING)

Gaps between the
three levels -
Our Fatal Flaw

BRAINSTEM
(SENSATIONS)

Triangle Diagram

This book is based on the concept that, when it comes to understanding the psychological brain, there are three distinctly different levels of functioning. For most people this will be an entirely new way of looking at how the brain works, especially when dealing with mental disorders and also relationship problems.

To help explain this concept I have come up with the diagram on the facing page. The top triangle represents the prefrontal cortex of the human brain, which is the thinking or cognitive brain. It has one given area.

The middle tier represents the limbic system where we 'feel' our world, as distinct from thinking about it. Notice that the feeling area is three times the size of the thinking brain. In terms of psychological makeup, the feelings (three areas) have the power to over-ride the thinking brain (one area).

The bottom level represents our way of sensing the world, as different from feeling and thinking about it. This level is the very foundation of who we are as humans. Notice that it contains five areas. This does not mean the brainstem is five times bigger in volume than the thinking brain, as that is obviously not the case. The difference in area relates to the inherent power that each part of the brain has, especially in relation as to how it affects the levels it is adjacent to. For example sensations and feelings combined have a tremendous ability to overwhelm the thinking mind. However the thinking mind has very little influence over the feelings, and this action comes to the fore when we suffer overwhelming emotions (e.g. it is difficult to think our way out of depression or a panic attack). The difference of power and function between the levels is very important in understanding the human condition. It can explain almost all psychological disorders that the human race is suffering from.

When the imprints in the lower levels are mostly from traumatic experiences, rather than loving ones, the awfulness of the feelings that are generated have to be kept from conscious awareness at the top level. Hence the brain creates a disconnection, or gap, between the sensations and feelings, and also between the feelings and cognition.

These gaps in functioning create our fatal flaw because, although they are designed to keep primal pain repressed, that same action also blocks access to our loving feelings. These actions are subconscious and are so effective that hardly anybody is aware of how much primal pain they carry, or of how powerful the feeling of love can be when unencumbered by pain.

As you read this book keep this diagram in mind and also the one on the front cover, as it will help you understand the concepts in this book.

THE IMPRINT

One of the most important components of the fatal flaw in the human brain is the power of the imprints. One definition of a psychological imprint is as follows (taken from the web at medicenenet.com) *an imprint is a remarkable phenomenon that occurs in animals and theoretically in humans, in the first hours of life. The newborn creature bonds to the types of animals it meets at birth and begins to pattern its behaviour after them. In humans this is often called bonding and usually refers to the relationship between the newborn and its parent.* Another definition from Wikipedia is --- *To learn something indelibly at a particular stage in life.* The definition of primal imprinting could be a combination of the two and yet it would still fall short of describing the importance of imprints in psychological disorders and also in peoples' everyday lives.

Imprints generate an incredibly strong force that is at the forefront of nearly all of humanity's problems. The force of these sensations is not factored into the current approach the psych's have in their understanding of the causes and cures of mental illness. To get some understanding of the strength of this force we need to go back into our evolutionary history.

At this stage of the discussion I may be losing readers who believe in God and Creation and not evolution. My own thoughts on the matter are that creation and evolution are the same things. If a sea slug develops into many other species, one of which is Homo Sapiens, then is that creation or not? I am not being flippant in my views because the creation versus evolution debate causes a great divide within the human species. It is one of the issues we humans need to resolve so that we can all live in peace, or if we cannot resolve the issue, at least discuss it in a rational manner. Either way, evolution or creation, it is not an issue that should be dividing communities, and certainly not worth killing each other over.

Now back to the sea slug that lived on the ocean floor some five hundred million years ago. The slug like body had a canal running through it that had an opening (mouth) and an exit point (anus). In between these two points the canal was the place where food was digested and the required nutrients absorbed into the body and the waste passed on through. This part of the animal body has remained pretty much the same, and although the modern day digestive system is a lot more sophisticated, it still serves the same purpose.

At this stage of our development, we also had a rudimentary nervous system that controlled our minimal body movements. These two systems are intricately involved in our human physiology today. The most well known is the 'gut feeling' or intuition that more often than not proves correct. This happens because the nervous system works things out subconsciously and lets us know through the feelings in the 'gut', and this system has been tested for its dependability over millions of years.

The physical act of vomiting can also be a reaction to an extremely nervous or emotional situation. One interesting thing about undergoing primal therapy is that some of my most traumatic moments of childhood were expressed as an 'energy vomit'. The nervousness would start in my lower stomach, around the naval area, and over time and with a great deal of effort and emotion, this energy would explode out through my mouth or top of my head. The physical body has the vomit reflex that ejects poisonous or unwanted physical substances from the stomach, but the same reflex will also expel unwanted 'emotional' experiences, or what some might call bad psychic energy.

The body and nervous system evolved to the stage of what we now call the reptilian brain, or brainstem. The alligator (a reptile) is known as an evolutionary successful species that lives by sensations alone. All of the alligators' survival instincts are imprinted in a brain that is the human equivalent of a brainstem only. The human species went on to develop a limbic system that turned sensations into feeling, and then a cortex that turned feelings into thoughts. In regard to this process it is important to understand that the limbic and cortical areas of the brain formed out of the influence of the forces generated by the brainstem sensations. Antonio Demasio is a neuroscientist who wrote a book called 'Descartes Error'. In this book he describes the process of brain evolution from brainstem, to limbic, to cortex, with the lower levels controlling how the upper levels developed. The brainstem always maintained control because it kept the organism alive, therefore it could not allow itself to be over-ruled by higher brain structures.

This developmental process means the imprints in the brainstem drive what we feel, and then feelings drive what we think – or for the purposes of explaining the fatal flaw in the human brain, feelings drive what we believe. The information flow is mostly one way, in that sensation has a huge impact on the cognitive mind, but ideas and beliefs from the cognitive mind do not flow down to exert influence on the sensations. This is why Cognitive Behaviour type therapies are notoriously ineffective. (some UK studies give an ineffective rate of around forty percent).

The above concept is such an important part of understanding the fatal flaw and mental disorders that I will explain it again in a slightly different way.

We first evolved a brainstem that sensed its environment. The brainstem sensations alone could maintain life, much as they do in modern day reptiles. Eventually we developed a limbic system that could register feeling, but this part of our brain developed slowly from our brainstem, so sensations were turned into feeling. We did not evolve feelings separately, they came from the output of our sensations.

The last level to evolve was the cortex and this area developed with the underlying input of our feelings. In the same way that feelings evolved from sensation, so our cognitive brain evolved out of our feelings.

The only way to fully appreciate this action of the brain is to experience it firsthand. In my case it was by undergoing primal therapy. The therapy starts by addressing any act-outs. All neurotic behaviours and irrational beliefs are classed as act-outs in primal therapy because we are acting- out our primal pain rather than turning inward and facing it. During therapy act-outs are forbidden and the person is directed to their feelings instead.

The underlying feeling, which is usually painful, is brought into conscious awareness and dealt with. As my own therapy progressed I found myself going deeper into sensations, so I experienced my feelings as coming from powerful sensations. As I experienced the sensations I also realized they came from imprints. Dealing with painful imprints and the sensations they generate is the deepest of all healing processes.

As the healing process unfolded my psychological problems dropped away and my belief system was largely dismantled. People say to me "It sounds like primal theory and therapy is your belief system now." But I can only reply that my belief system has been replaced with a sensing/ feeling system, which is an entirely different thing. One of the major differences between the two is that a belief system has the capacity to disrespect and even kill other humans, whereas a healthy sensing/ feeling system holds true to the principals of pure love.

In my book *'Love, Sex and Mental Health'* I describe this process using the analogy of a three story house. The penthouse represents the cortex, the living rooms the limbic system and the basement represents the brainstem. The basement and its foundations determine the size and strength of the rest of the house above it. In my case a poor foundation caused my whole house to tumble down around me, represented by a depressive breakdown in actual life. The process of primal therapy took me from my penthouse, down through the feelings rooms and into the basement.

Using the house analogy I can explain why the psych industry does not fully understand the causes of mental illness. Learning to be a psychologist or psychiatrist involves mostly the thinking brain, with only a cursory understanding of feelings and emotions. That means they stay in their penthouse trying to work out why things are going wrong. During their own therapy they may sometimes enter the feeling rooms but not descend far enough down the steps to experience the deeper layers. The journey needs to continue downwards through their feeling rooms and into the basement, where they would get to experience an actual sensation and from this come to understand the power of the imprint. I strongly emphasize that this needs to be an experience, because it is not something that can be understood from reading a book.

In my experience when a primal patient is in the basement of their mind they have absolutely no doubt that all psychological disorders are caused by poor parenting practices. Once again I am not trying to blame parents as such; every parent wants the best for their children, but our cultural lack of understanding of the power of the imprint and what love actually is, is part of humanity's fatal flaw.

Within the current mental health paradigm talking therapies are a large part of any treatment plan for mental disorders. Any person who has ever experienced the power of their imprints will understand that talk therapies will not touch an imprint. Cognitive Behavioural Therapists are coming up with many different ways of treating mental illness, but the underlying process of using talk therapies keeps the patient in their cortex, or penthouse, when the problem is in the brainstem, or basement. Some of these therapies show results, but that is achieved by altering symptoms, not by eliminating the cause.

Psychotherapy understands that emotions are important, and dealing with them in a treatment plan can have positive effects. However emotions are not the same as feelings and sensations. These types of therapies start the journey to deeper healing but go nowhere near far enough. Using the analogy of the house, they enter the stairway from the penthouse into the feeling rooms, but only take a few steps down before going back up into the penthouse to do an analysis of what they found. This analysis by the therapist can make people feel a little better because they now understand some of their problem, but understanding is not a cure. The imprint in the basement remains untouched and keeps giving off sensations that wreak havoc in the feeling rooms and penthouse.

I will now discuss a few recent and relevant articles I have read to highlight the power of the imprint and how the current mental health paradigm misses this important aspect of brain functioning. The following is an article from New Scientist 15th March 2014.

Part 1.

"Cognitive tests and brain scans suggest addiction and obsessive compulsive disorder (OCD) share a lack of control of behaviour."

Comment. Lack of control of behaviour is the power of the imprint being too strong for the cognitive mind to over-ride.

Part 2.

"Individuals with OCD performed much like gambling addicts, suggesting their underlying brain problems may be similar."

Comment. This supports primal theory in the understanding that all psychological disorders have a similar underlying cause; which is lack of love early in life. Although childhood trauma is by far the main cause, trauma that is unresolved can also occur later in life, such as with Post Traumatic Stress Disorder (PTSD).

Part 3.

"OCD sufferers get anxious if they can't complete their rituals. OCD is usually treated as an anxiety disorder with talking therapies to relieve distress, or anti anxiety drugs. These approaches reduce symptoms but only a minority of people are cured."

Comment. In primal theory terms this explains that act-outs (the rituals) help to keep the anxious feelings repressed. In therapy the act-outs are stopped and then the rising anxiety is followed down into the brainstem (basement) where it is usually experienced as incredible terror. Under the current paradigm OCD is treated either with talk therapy or drugs. Drugs block the connection between the imprints and the cortex. They can reduce the messaging but they do not eliminate the source.

In the final sentence the psych's admit these approaches reduce symptoms but cure only a minority of people. This fact appears to be true of so many psychological problems. The causes are not understood and so treatment methods that do not address the causes produce less than ideal results.

This next discussion is from an article posted on the internet and the headline reads, 'Anxious kids suffer in silence: professor.'

Article. *"One or two children in every Australian classroom is too anxious to enjoy life, says a professor who is concerned problems often go unnoticed by parents and teachers."*

Comment. At this stage the psychology industry has no way of reliably measuring how anxious anybody is, including adults. Things like anxiety and depression can go unnoticed for several reasons. Firstly the sufferer can mask their problems by smiling and getting on with life; have you ever heard the expression 'the smiling depression'.

Secondly, from my own experience, people do not really know what the problem is and are too scared to say anything about what ails them.

Thirdly, if a person has lived with mild anxiety and/or depression all their lives, they can mistake this state of mind as being normal. It was certainly the case with me. We do not yet have a real way of measuring a child's anxiety levels so I would say that only one or two children per classroom is a very conservative estimate.

Article. *"Some children are overlooked because they are conscientious students and it is difficult to know they are constantly worrying, says Ron Rapee, Professor of Psychology at Macquarie University."*

Comment. Conscientious students can have a high IQ which is a measure of the cognitive brain, but the psych profession does not have a measure of the activity or capability of the lower brain. The imprinted sensations in the lower brain cause the constant worrying. The child is forced to be continually on the alert because their early environment was not safe.

Article. *"Common concerns include a fear of making mistakes, always being on time, family finances, health, crime, friendships or being laughed at."*

Comment. Fear of making mistakes is one of the most common issues that primal patients encounter during therapy. It comes from parents who apply too much discipline, not enough freedom to explore, and punish children when they make mistakes. Pushing a child to excel in school also makes them anxious. Our culture places a lot more emphasis on a high IQ and academic grades, which are prefrontal cortex activities, rather than on social functioning, which are limbic and brainstem functions.

Article. *"The children might always expect the worst, suffer stomach pain and headaches and have trouble sleeping, says Prof Rapee, who is director of the Centre for Emotional Health at the university."*

Comment. They always expect the worst because that's what they got earlier in life, and now their imprinting is warning them to be careful, regardless of the present day circumstances. I am also writing from my own personal experience. Stomach pains, headaches and sleeping disorders can all be symptoms of traumatic imprinting. As I explained earlier, anxiety is experienced in our digestive system because these two systems evolved together early in evolution.

Article. *"But the strongest indicator of anxiety is avoidance. Most anxious children have a range of things that they just refuse to do."*

Comment. Avoidance of what we fear is a common way of dealing with anxiety, even for adults. OCD sufferers get anxious if they cannot carry out their rituals, and others need their drug of choice.

Article. *"The central problem is they fear people will think badly of them"*, *says Prof Rapee who is running a workshop on childhood anxiety at a College of Clinical Psychologists Conference in Melbourne.*

Comment. This feeling is most probably from an imprint and will affect the child's relationships for the rest of their lives. If children sensed their parents didn't like them, they rationalise this situation by believing "It was my fault, I must have been bad". Then they go through life with an imprint that constantly grinds out the sensation that everyone will think I am bad.

Article. *"His aim is to teach colleagues how to use the university's Cool Kids program to help children aged between seven and seventeen, and their families. 'Most anxious children can be helped,' he says."*

Comment. It is true that most anxious children can be helped to some degree, but nothing that approaches a cure. Once again it is only fiddling with the symptoms of a disorder, while the cause goes unrecognised and therefore not dealt with.

Article. *"Parents can start with basic common sense procedures like talking to the child about the evidence for their worries and gradually encouraging the child to do the things they are afraid of doing, he says."*

Comment. From a primal theory perspective, my own personal

experience and also from current research such as the Adverse Childhood Experience (ACE) it is highly likely the parents caused the problem in the first place. Retraining parents, as the article suggests, is a good place to start, but this does not tell us why our collective parenting skills are so poor in the first place.

Article. *"If necessary, parents can ask a GP for a referral to a clinical psychologist or use Kool Kids resources to coach their own children. Children living in Sydney can attend sessions at the centre."*

Comment. In a loving society good parenting will come naturally and children will not suffer these sorts of problems. The above action is once again trying to change symptoms caused by deep-seated imprinting.

Article. *"Anxious children often exaggerate the danger or catastrophise the situation. 'We teach them to consider if there is evidence for what they are worrying about', says Prof Rapee."*

Comment. This statement can only be made by a person who has not experienced the power of early imprints. Chronic anxiety is usually traced back to the experience of sheer terror at the brainstem level. We all have needs as babies, one of which is safety. If our lives are threatened by things like getting stuck in the birth canal, or our parents constantly fight between themselves, or we get belted for slight misdemeanours, then the terror of experiencing *"my life is in danger"* becomes catastrophic and that reaction is imprinted into the brainstem. When a similar feeling of not being safe occurs in the present, the brain reacts in the same way it did originally. The reaction may not be appropriate for the current situation, but that is how the brain works. Trying to tell a child its fear is unfounded is not supporting the child in understanding its feelings, and this is a big mistake because 'feeling' is who we are at our very core, and not acknowledging a child's feelings is the same as not acknowledging the child.

Article. *"The program gets children to face their fears in a systematic way. They gradually confront things they are fearful off. However, it's important for parents not to over-react to every child's worries".*

Comment. Facing the object of our terror, like getting closer to snakes and spiders, has some effect on altering symptoms, but does not touch the imprint. During primal therapy we deal with our fears by facing the original imprint, which is a very scary thing to do, but the pay-off is that we can live a less fearful life naturally.

Article. *"Anxiety is a natural emotion. All children will go through periods of being anxious. What we are looking for is where the anxiety goes on for long periods and where it interferes with a child's life. "*

Comment. Anxiety is a natural emotion, with an underlying feeling of fear, but it should never stop us from enjoying our lives. When this happens you can be sure it is imprinted terror from past fearful and life threatening experiences.

Our present day fears and phobias may not be directly related to anything in our past. Imprinted fears are more likely to be projected onto present day objects or situations that appear mundane to other people. Severely anxious people are usually afraid of most things in their lives, not just one or two specific things.

Imprints and brain development

There is increasing evidence showing that a child's early environment and imprinting can help shape certain areas of the brain, and that these areas are implicated in the process of mental disorders. To put that in primal terms it is the power of the imprint in the brainstem that shapes these developing brain areas, especially the limbic and pre-frontal cortex.

A recent (2015) German/Italian rodent study highlighted the capability of the lower brain structures to influence other brain areas. The researchers stated that these findings should inform other researchers in attention and behaviour studies, especially when investigating causes of certain attention and behaviour difficulties.

Anxiety and the amygdalae.

Changes in the development of the amygdalae, which is known as the fear centre of the brain, appear to make children more likely to be angry. Stanford University researchers did MRI scanning on 76 children aged 7, 8 and 9. The children with high levels of anxiety all had larger amygdalae, which was also better connected with brain regions that look after attention and emotional perception and regulation. From a primal theory perspective this would most probably mean they are more alert because they see their environment fearfully.

Imprints and addictions

Researchers from Penn State University, including assistant Professor Stephen Wilson, put smokers on a functional magnetic resonance imaging (FMRI) machine, and those with the most addictive tendencies had weaker responses in the brains ventral striatum. (The ventral striatum is well known as being part of the brains reward system).

Comment. Could it be that an unloved person develops a weaker than average reward system because that system is not activated early in life? Too much fear, criticism and/or just disinterested parenting will not activate the reward system, and so it remains small for life. Then we eventually find a substance or activity that gives us a small feeling of reward and we become addicted. The above article was on the internet where people could post comments on people with addictions. One such comment was "*I have one thing to say – try a little willpower-stop being weak and looking for excuses*". Obviously this person does not know willpower is a function of the cognitive brain only and that addiction gets its power from the brainstem. This puts our willpower in a battle against brainstem imprints which makes it a very one-sided and hopeless affair.

Alzheimer's and the caudate nucleus

A 2013 study has suggested a link between patients with Alzheimers and the caudate nucleus. MRI images were used to measure the volume of the caudate nucleus in Alzheimer's and normal volunteers, with the Alzheimer's patients showing a significant reduction in volume. The caudate nucleus is also implicated in Parkinson's disease, in that the nigrostriatal track shows depletion of dopamine carrying neurons. Schizophrenia, Obsessive Compulsive Disorder and ADHD all have abnormalities of the caudate nucleus, which is also part of the pleasure pathway. Could it be that not getting our needs for love met early in life leads to an under-developed pleasure pathway and an over-developed fear pathway.

Imprints and choice

"Violence is a choice" exclaimed a man from the television show I was watching. He also claimed that humans are violent by nature, but it can be controlled because of our cognitive brain.

The above comments show a flaw in human reasoning. The brainstem is the most powerful or influential part of the human brain, and when the pressure is on and split-second decisions are made, the brainstem reacts from imprinted history before the cognitive mind knows what is going on.

A loving person is not violent. They have the moral strength and ability to defend themselves and others from attack if necessary, but at other times they are loving people who other people feel safe being around. They have a healthy brainstem that reacts in appropriate ways without needing cognitive control.

Article on anger in New Scientist 9th February, 2013.

"The effect on their relationship is clear. Their children, wives, bosses and families are frightened of them and they scare everyone away," says Mike Fisher, director of the British Association of Anger Management based in East Grinstead. *"You can't believe the number of people we get like that. They have no friends. Their family has left. All they do is work or act out with a whole variety of addictions. Whatever the causes, there is no cure for excessive anger. A person who feels inappropriately angry must generally always work to manage it."*

From a primal theory viewpoint anger is generated from a hurt. When our needs are not met as a child we tend to get angry, as any child throwing a tantrum will show. Our culture usually deals with tantrums by punishment, when we should be asking the child what is going on with their feelings. It is awesome watching an adult throwing a tantrum during their therapy - one they should have been allowed to express as a child. After enough anger is expressed the patient is able to feel the original hurt, and as the hurt is expressed the angry outbursts will reduce. Most violent acts in our culture today stem from past hurts, and so people can lash out at others at the smallest of provocations.

The imprint and our inability to have a choice in our actions also plays out in addictions. I believe a loving person has no addictions. They have no need for drugs, alcohol or cigarettes, because they already have good feelings flowing through their bodies; they do not need artificial aids to get the dopamine and oxytocins flowing, which are the common hormones in the pleasure pathway. When they feel hungry they eat good wholesome food, not some junk food that satisfies an inner need for comfort. Every addict will tell you that they cannot control their addiction, whatever it may be. They have the trouble of self control because the imprint of pain in the brainstem is the controlling force, and their addictions help keep the pain repressed.

The same primal force is at work in paedophilia. Newspaper reports often quote the convicted felon as saying *"I could not control my impulses"*. This comment is the crux of the whole problem but it gets lost in the context of the crime. My own experience with a worrisome deviant sexual feeling leads me to believe paedophilia is the result of an inappropriately imprinted brain.

In all these cases people do not really have a choice, because the power of the imprint is too strong. They may know what they are doing is wrong, or not healthy, or not in the best interests of others, but there is nothing they can do about it. Nobody chooses to be depressed, angry, anxious, or to suffer from schizophrenia or bi-polar, or to be a narcissist or psychopath. These conditions are all shaped by imprinted pain. People in their right minds would never choose any of these ways of being in the world, especially if we had some way of experiencing true love.

For example, a narcissist or psychopath may say they have good lives; everything is fine in their life, its other people who are the problem! Firstly they do not understand what damage they do to other people when expressing their neurotic behaviour, and secondly, if they have never experienced a truly loving life, then how would they know the difference. Sinead O'Connor is an Irish songstress who sings, in her powerful voice 'if you never had a good time how would you recognise one.' This knowledge is an important outcome of primal therapy. I have experienced a life with a huge load of primal pain, and now that most of the pain has gone, I experience life in a different way, and that difference is truly remarkable. Previous to my therapy I was aware my life was missing something, but had no idea what it was, and that it would change my life so dramatically when I found it.

The belief in our culture that we have unrestricted choices is stifling our understanding of a greater and deeper problem with human functioning. Positive Psychologists and Cognitive Behavioural Therapists base their treatment plans on the understanding that we have choices in the way we think and behave. But this approach does not come close to factoring in the power of the imprints in influencing the choices we make in our lives.

The number of self help books in the market place is astronomical, but the basic message in all of them is in using the thinking mind to create change. The books all have the same protocol in that the first action is to sit down and read the book and then get busy doing what the book advises, which mostly involves trying to change your attitude and actions. Changing your diet, taking up meditation, physical exercise, positive thinking and many other of the spiritual based practises are using the cognitive mind to try and reduce symptoms. Despite all these books and the advice being available, many indicators suggest that mental health problems are on the increase. That is because none of these activities deal with the actual imprints directly, and the imprints are the reason why so many of these attempts at improving a person's life are not successful. The cognitive solutions that have some success only work because they shift a person's focus away from unpleasant feelings.

As a contrast good primal therapy takes a person deep into their brain. We go into a padded room with a therapist where we are encouraged to start feeling with the aim of eventually dealing with imprinted traumatic memories and their related pain. The therapist will never suggest any cognitive course of action, because they know that when the patient feels the original imprinted trauma, they also regain their own personal power. When we become a sensing/feeling human being exuding love from a permanently 'repaired' brainstem, all the wonderful things the self help books' tell us about will happen in a natural and easy way.

Imprints can also be a powerful factor in our work choices. Most of the greatest musicians and composers were born into family environments that were full of music. Many of the best chefs either come from families who had restaurants, or the parents were good cooks and mealtimes were pleasant family gatherings. This is how imprints are supposed to work in a positive way. We are born into a certain culture and the imprint becomes a strong auto pilot for the rest of our lives.

As a contrast I was born into a house with no music, the meals were very basic, and when my father cooked I had trouble eating the mush he served up. Mealtimes were commonly a frightening experience, because mum and dad would sometimes be fighting, the days punishments were often handed out, and trying to choke down ghastly pearl barley soaked in animal fat was not a pleasant experience.

That is not to say any particular person cannot be successful as a chef or musician if they haven't been imprinted along those lines, but my observations over a lifetime would suggest it makes life easier if they have been.

Imprints and phantom pain.
I have known of many people who have had physical pains checked out by specialists, only to be told they can't find anything physically wrong. Typical areas are stomach, chest and head pains and also dizziness. During primal therapy a lot of these pains resolve themselves. For example when someone is reliving the grief of not being loved by parents, they will experience crushing chest pain, and when they have done enough reliving their day to day chest pains will disappear. These phantom pains can be parts of a memory of a previous traumatic experience that has not been dealt with at the level of the imprint. Imprinting and how at effects the three levels of consciousness will help to understand the phenomenon of phantom pain.

Also through my experiences I have an understanding of how healthy brainstem imprints are necessary for a healthy physical body - the mind/body connection. The medical profession are heavily into treating many of humanity's physical problems, without understanding the basic causes. For example, after undergoing extensive primal therapy, I believe that most cancers and heart disease are the result of faulty lifestyle choices that are driven by the imprints of a traumatised brainstem.

The imprint is involved in almost all cases of physical and mental ill health and yet under the current zeitgeist its power goes mostly unrecognised.

THE GLOBAL AREA OF LOVE (GAL) SCORE

In my previous book 'Love Sex and Mental Health' I wrote a chapter about the need for a human global area of love (GAL) score. This proposed GAL score also provides a scale with which to measure a person's level of mental health, something that is much needed within the psychology industry. I will do a short summary here for those who have not read that book.

The common Intelligence Quotient (IQ) score is a well known measure of brain functioning. As the title suggests it only measures intelligence, and intelligence is mostly a measure of the cognitive brain. But primal theory says we have two other parts of our brain, the brainstem sensations and the limbic system feelings that have a powerful influence on our lives, and especially so on our relationships. Neuroscientists who do brain scans tell us that parts of the limbic system, especially the amygdalae, are active during emotional states. The locus ceruleus of the brainstem also lights up during the fear response.

Psych's are also puzzled as to why many quite intelligent people can be so socially inept. The common profile of the mad professor is such an example. The professor has a high IQ and is brilliant in his job, but almost totally dysfunctional in relationships with others.

I have proposed a scoring system for the lower brains to measure social functioning, and as love is powerfully implicit in this type of functioning I called it the Global Area of Love (GAL) score. Psychology has a score for emotional intelligence that they refer to as the EQ score. However, as I try to explain in this book, emotions come after sensations and feelings, emotions being the part of a reaction we can notice or see at the surface. Underneath the emotions are feelings and then lower down are the sensations. Any therapy that requires a person to manage their emotions is likely not formed from the understanding that the force of the emotions is driven by the imprints in the brainstem.

The problem now becomes what measures to use in determining a person's GAL score, because love in our culture is still a very subjective experience.

The brainstem controls a lot of our biological states so biological measures would be included in determining a persons' GAL score. These would include heart rate, blood pressure and stress hormones. A system that is constantly under pressure from primal pain is like a car engine that is over-revving. The engine will wear out quicker because its parts are moving faster than they need to for optimum performance. In a human body under pressure the heart rate, blood pressure and stress hormones are all elevated. As a consequence a high percentage of the western world's population are on blood pressure tablets to reduce the pressure on the heart or they take medications like Prozac or Zoloft to calm down an over-stressed system.

The following article appeared in the West Australian newspaper 24th April 2014. The headline read 'Heart test for mental disorders'. *A radical new medical test will measure patients' heart rates to determine if they have a mental illness....* and later in the article.... *A team lead by Western Australian psychiatrist Dr Stephen Addis uncovered distinct patterns in the heart rate data of depression sufferers as well as those suffering other mental disorders.* And this result from an Italian study on rodents. *'Currently depression is diagnosed only by its symptoms, but the results put us on track to discover signatures in humans that may have potential to serve as markers for certain types of depression.* (Neurotrophic factors and CNS disorders: finding in rodent models of depression and schizophrenia. F. Angelucci, P. Math, L Aloe). From a primal theory perspective both these tests could provide biological markers that help to determine a person's GAL score. These two examples are only a start and I am sure scientists will find many more biological markers when they know what they are looking for, or start to interpret what they have already found in terms of a GAL score.

It is already known that the average life span of a person with a mental illness is lower than the general population. Primal theory understands this phenomenon in terms of an over-revving system that wears out quicker. Some say it is because mentally ill patients are more likely to suicide, abuse alcohol and cigarettes, take more risks and consume illegal drugs, but all these things are symptoms of a larger underlying disease. So the severity of any psychological disorder could also be used to determine a GAL score. For example there are already many diagnostic levels for depression and anxiety. Primal theory says that the greater the intensity of depression and/or anxiety, the larger the pool of primal pain is likely to be. As the pool of primal pain increases so does the level of repression, and the heavier the repression the less we can feel love.

My proposed GAL score has a scale of 1 to 100, with 100 being the best of human functioning score possible. From my personal experience there would be two scores within this range that have special significance. The first one is a score of 50 because this is where the person is very neurotic but still has some form of reality, even if that reality is largely distorted. They can still function at some level in daily life. Below this score the person has so much primal pain that they become increasingly psychotic. That means they are leaving any semblance of an objective reality behind, to live in a subjective reality where there is no pain. This state of mind is where a person becomes dysfunctional in their daily lives. They have severe problems with relationships and jobs, and many of them end up living a heavily medicated life, or in jail and mental institutions. Common diagnosis for these people would be severe Bipolar, Borderline Personality Disorder and Schizophrenia.

Another score of significance is 80. This is the level of feeling required to produce oxytocin, and therefore have the ability to feel love, especially with a partner. Below this level sex can feel good, but it is driven only by testosterone. The human body needs to produce oxytocin to allow bonding to happen, both to your partner and to your children, especially during and directly after childbirth.

Michel Odent is a French Doctor who understands the necessity for humans to have a natural birth, and for a flow of natural oxytocin that allows a mother and baby's bonding physiology to occur. Dr Odent says that many mothers are unable to produce enough natural oxytocins, and I would suggest this is so because their GAL scores are well below 80. As a persons' GAL score drops - meaning that the system is repressing more primal pain - other natural bodily systems also become repressed, including the birth process, sexual expression, the immune system and even digestion.

With a score of 80 or above a person will have only minor and fleeting psychological disorders. They do not have much primal pain to repress so their reality is very objective and their persona reflects a loving disposition.

I believe that a future society will develop a measure of the lower brain, and it will become more important for that society to produce adults with a high GAL score rather than a high IQ. From the above explanations I believe a minimum GAL score of 80 for every person on this planet should be the ultimate aim of humanity. In actual fact this shift in understanding is happening in many places now. People are starting to realise that the materialistic and technological society we have developed does not fulfil human need.

In Germany they have done research on the development of children in kindergartens. In the short term, kindergartens that focus on intellectual learning and testing produce brighter children, but the effect only lasts for a few years. The children in kindergartens who focus on play and adventure turn out to be higher achieving and better adjusted as adults.

The above research supports primal theory in as much as we are first and foremost social animals, and so our children's social brains should be nurtured more than their intellectual brains. I feel it is worth pointing out to the 'Tiger' mums (those who push their children to achieve academically) out there that an unloved brainstem will be imprinted in a negative way, and then negativity, brain chatter, depression, phobias and anxiety will interfere in the processes of the cognitive mind. Psychological disorders of all kinds have ruined many promising academic or intellectual careers.

At this stage the use of a GAL score is useful for me to illustrate some concepts in this book. For example if you look at the chart in the appendix, you will see how human functioning decreases as the GAL score decreases, and eventually gets to a stage where we can start killing each other, particularly with our massive war machines. However there are many other subtle and indirect ways that our 'fatal flaw' can be deadly to our fellow humans.

The Three Pillars of a
Healthy Life

I would suggest that there are three main areas of human existence that are vitally important for living a happy and healthy life. They are the ability to give and receive love, combined with good nutrition and daily exercise. My reasons for selecting these three areas have a lot to do with the way we evolved. Our modern day society appears to be a lot more complex than that, but when it is stripped of its complexity our basic needs for survival are covered by love, food and exercise.

Billions of dollars have been spent on research trying to find ways to make us all healthier and happier, but despite this massive effort, most parameters suggest we are sliding deeper in to the mire of ill-health.

Much of modern day research is proving that the way we used to live fifty thousand years ago is the way we should be living now. Obviously our technological advances have changed how we live, where we live and given us many other benefits and comforts. Even so, at the core of our being, the need for love, good food and regular exercise has not diminished. The fatal flaw in our brains has allowed us to wander away from these three basic requirements. The human race has become bedazzled with its technological marvels, and where humans are suffering or having problems we think our intellectual abilities will save the day.

A good example is the hope that scientists are putting into genetics to cure many illnesses, both physical and mental, and yet this science is not yet proven. We also seem to be waiting for the next wonder drug to cure cancer, obesity, heart problems and many other disease states. Meanwhile our inability to love, eat good food and get regular exercise is causing many illnesses that make a human existence miserable, as well as shortening many lives.

Wars are one obvious way that the fatal flaw in the human brain is deadly to people, but the lifestyles we have adopted are also killing people at earlier ages than necessary, and in ever increasing numbers. To make my case I will discuss each of the three pillars in more detail.

Love (pillar number one)

Love is a very strong force and it has many aspects to it that relate to how we live in this world. Lack of being able to love causes social isolation, and social isolation is involved in many disease processes.

This article appeared in the West Australian newspaper on 25th May 2012. The headline reads 'Being home alone poses alarming threat to health – New research unearths the hidden dangers of social isolation.' My first cynical reaction was the thought that I had read many similar research reports over my lifetime, and why are they wasting research dollars on such common knowledge. Why aren't people doing something about the situation rather than doing more research?

In my opinion this over-researching is widespread in both the social and health sciences, and I believe it exists because the causes of problems cannot be uncovered with the current research methods that ignore the power of the first level of consciousness. So researchers seem stuck in the process of forever researching symptoms without ever understanding causes. It is all well and good to research the fact that social isolation causes increased risk of disease, but what are the causes of social isolation?

However I will use this latest research to show how social isolation can kill us, just as surely as bullets and bombs can.

Article. "Social isolation has detrimental health effects similar to smoking 15 cigarettes a day, or six alcoholic drinks, and more detrimental than no exercise and/or obesity. Living alone has been linked to significant mental health problems such as depression, suicide, sleeplessness, and propensity for suicide – on the physical side it has also been linked to high blood pressure. The researchers warned there were indications that people were becoming more socially isolated, despite technology and globalisation that would presumably foster social connections."

My comment. In the last sentence we have the effect of the fatal flaw in human thinking. The real problem is we are becoming more socially isolated because of technology and globalisation, not despite it. One of the problems with technology is that in our mad rush to push the boundaries of our thinking minds, we have ignored the importance of our social brains in making our lives worth living. That is why we need to understand the brain from all three levels of consciousness, and to have some measure of the functioning of the social brain as separate from the thinking brain (such as my proposed GAL score). We have evolved to communicate face to face, so that we can read facial expressions and nuances of speech. Our social brains respond to other social brains nearby, possibly by using recently discovered 'mirror' neurons. The common text message, emails and Facebook have none of that, so they are a cold way to communicate.

I have friends and family who I communicate with once in awhile via the internet, but what I really need is someone who I can communicate with face to face, and on a daily basis. That is what long term marriage partners and close available friends do for each other.

Article. *"Fewer people are getting married, and divorce is more prevalent across all ages."*

My comment. As humans we are losing the ability to love. I would suggest the average GAL score is declining, making us more neurotic and therefore hard to get on with. Our feeling brains need loving social contact to thrive; that's how we evolved and no amount of technological advances will change that situation. The article mentions older people, especially women, as being at risk of social isolation. But humanity's inability to understand the true force of love and how it is needed to socialize our children from the first days of their lives, is the reason why these children become bitter and hard to get on with in their later years.

Personally I know of many cases where the grandparent, parent and older child/teenager relationship has completely broken down. These three-generational relationships should be the cornerstone of a loving community. On an individual basis being able to communicate and socialize effectively gives life its joy and meaning.

A needy child will spend its whole life trying to fulfil its need to be loved, and they end up as 'needy' grandparents. A needy senior can be a bitter and obnoxious person and therefore difficult to be around. They may suffer social isolation, but they are inadvertently the cause of their own problems.

From the Harvard University Grant Study (lead researcher George Vaillant) *'There is no doubt that evolution has shaped us to love one another. Loving relationships help our brains to develop, integrate and remain flexible, and when the drive to love is thwarted, when we are frightened, abused, or neglected – our mental health is compromised'.*

Blue Zones

Dan Buettner has written several books on places that are classed as Blue Zones. A Blue Zone is where the local population have less health problems and live to an older age when compared to other areas. One such place is a Greek Island called Ikaria, where Buettner reports in his book there is 20% less cancer, 50% less cardiovascular disease and almost no dementia. Apart from getting daily exercise by having to walk around a mountainous area and eating wild greens that have high antioxidant levels, they also have a rich and active social life.

The pace of life is slow and time is taken to connect with family and friends. On the weekends communities come together to eat and dance, with all age groups taking part. When interviewed by researchers, no-one reports feeling alone, and no-one feels useless. These people appear to be living closer to the way our ancestors lived, in that they have a good social life, they get regular exercise as part of their survival routine, and eat healthier, natural foods. Other Blue Zones include Okinawa and Sardinia, with the main common denominator being the quality of social life. In all cases the older people enjoyed the company of the younger ones, and they still felt like a useful part of the community.

In many societies today the move is toward segregation of the age groups. Pre-schoolers are herded into day-care centres, where the emphasis is becoming more focused on preparing the child for a successful academic career rather than being involved in creative play with people of various ages. School age children spend the majority of their day in rooms full of people their own age. Within schools the IQ remains supreme, because our 'emotional' life is a vague concept, and has even been regarded as a nuisance, especially when anxiety, depression and overstimulation (ADHD) get in the way of academic learning.

Teenagers and young adults go to nightclubs and parties where there are very few older people to oversee the safety of the younger ones. The middle years are spent working long hours to support a family, buy a house, and satisfy the needs of an economy based on consumerism. When retirement comes around it is becoming the accepted norm to live in a gated community or a retirement home.

When we socialize regularly in mixed age groups the younger members learn the lessons of life from the older people, and the older ones benefit from watching the younger ones develop through the stages of life, plus just enjoying each others' company. It is a well known fact in psychology that imitation is the most common form of learning, and we need communities who work and play together in mixed age groups for that to happen.

My own children and grandchildren let me know I am important in their lives, and they are certainly an important part of my life.

Food and nutrition (pillar number two)

While I was trying to sort out my own mental health problems I became interested in how food was often mentioned as being part of any possible cure. The natural approach to my life's problems seemed like an area worth investigating, so I decided to study Naturopathy. Anatomy and physiology were a large part of the first years of study, and I enjoyed learning how the human body is put together and how it works as a functioning unit.

First of all I learnt about the chemical level of organization, then the cellular level followed by the tissues, then the organ systems, such as heart, lung, kidneys and skin. So I learnt about how atoms and molecules make up chemicals, and then chemicals come together to form cells, and various types of cells make different types of tissues, and different types of tissues make up the organs. The next step was learning about bone tissue, the skeleton and the muscle systems that combine to give the human body the ability to move.

From there it was learning about the physiology of how the systems work, which included the nervous, lymphatic, digestive and reproductive systems. Perhaps the most useful thing I learned was the chemical composition of the body, and how that relates to the food we eat. There are three main substances that make up food and body parts, and we have all heard of fats, carbohydrates and proteins. The atoms that make these parts are carbon (C), oxygen (O), hydrogen (H) and nitrogen (N).

Carbohydrates

Carbohydrates make up only 2 or 3 percent of body weight and contain various amounts of C, H and O. They come in many forms and are commonly called sugars, starches, glycogen and cellulose. Glucose is a sugar that contains 6 carbon atoms, 12 hydrogen atoms and 6 oxygen atoms, usually represented like this -- $C_6 H_{12} O_6$. The main purpose of carbohydrates is to provide the energy source for the bodies activities, so although it only makes up a small percentage of body weight at any one time, it has a high turnover, which is the reason we need to eat so often. For those interested in weight control it is important to note that excess carbohydrates not used for immediate energy production are converted to fat. The modern diet contains too many processed carbohydrates, such as white sugar and white flour. The human body did not evolve on these processed foods.

Fats

Fats also are made up of C, H and O atoms but contain much less O, with palmitic acid having the formula $C16\ H32\ O2$. Fats in the body have the important use of storing energy in a condensed form. They can store 7 calories per gram while carbohydrates provide 4 calories per gram. Various types of fats are also used to make steroids such as cholesterol, sex hormones and bile salts. Other fat based molecules are involved in the allergic and inflammatory pathways. The modern diet generally contains too much fat, as well as the wrong mix of fats. It is important to eat some plant based fats that contain omega three's and sixes (unsaturated fats), and reduce reliance on animal fats (saturated).

We evolved eating animal fats but wild animals have a good percentage of unsaturated fats that suit the human dietary need. For example the Australian kangaroo has about fifteen percent unsaturated fats in its meat. Domesticated animals have very low levels of unsaturated fats, with intensely farmed and grain fed animals like cattle and chickens having almost zero amounts.

Food labellers and advertisers often use the public fear and misunderstanding of fats by saying a food is 98 per cent fat free. What they don't say is that the food is usually high in carbohydrates, and any carbs not burnt up by exercise or other bodily processes will end up as a saturated fat that is stored in the body. At some stage the person will need to eat a fat dense meal containing mixtures of the unsaturated fats that the body needs for optimum performance.

Protein

Proteins also have C, H and O as their base formula, but with the addition of N (nitrogen). Their functions in the body are many and varied, the main ones being structural such as collagen, skin, hair and fingernails, plus hormone production, muscle tissue, immune system, transport of other molecules, and as enzymes in many chemical reactions. All proteins can be obtained from food, but not all food contains the twenty types needed for the body. Meat sources of protein supply a complete set, but plant sources are deficient in some types, meaning that vegetarians need to eat a variety of foods to get a correct balance. Excess protein is also broken down and stored as fat, with the nitrogen leaving the body as urea in the urine.

During natural therapy classes I learnt that a good diet should contain about 55 per cent carbohydrates, 30 per cent protein and 15 per cent fats, with at least 5 per cent being unsaturated fats. Despite all the myriad diets that come and go, the large majority of research shows that the above ratios still form the basis of a healthy and sustainable diet. The important thing to know about these food groups and their specific chemical makeup is that they are interchangeable in the body. For example the body can take a sugar molecule made up of C, H and O and then add an N to make a required protein.

Vitamins such as A, the B group, the all important C, and the fat soluble D and E are also needed for optimum health. Some trace minerals are also important, with iron (blood) and calcium (bones) being commonest with potassium, sodium, magnesium and phosphorous being others. The vitamins and minerals needed by the body are also contained in the natural sources of carbohydrates, proteins and fats. For example almonds contain protein and good fats, and are also good sources of the B group vitamins and calcium. Bananas provide carbohydrates but are also rich in potassium and other electrolytes. Green leafy vegetables have folic acid, vitamin C and calcium, plus provide fibre for healthy bowel movement. Meat contains good quality protein and various amounts of fats, but also contains minerals like iron and copper.

My studies in Naturopathy placed a big emphasis on good nutrition in maintaining good health, and they supplied a list of rules to follow that have stood the test of time.

- Eat natural foods as fresh from nature as possible

- No processed foods

- Eat foods that are in season for your area

- Eat a variety of foods in moderation

- Reduce reliance on animal fats and proteins and replace with plant sources

- Eat some nuts and berries each day

- Plenty of green leafy vegetables

- No processed meats

During the nutrition classes we discussed many common diseases and their causes, and in nearly all cases the main approach was to change people's diet using the recommendations listed above. There were some variations to this approach, such as eating foods known to contain iron for those suffering anaemia, and in macular degeneration eating dark coloured berries because their polyphenol content helped in stopping further damage to the eyesight.   This was the time in my life where I came to understand how important diet was to good health, but I also wondered, if it was that simple, why do so many people continue to eat themselves to sickness and death?

The study of herbal medicines was also very interesting. All native cultures have knowledge of the medicinal plants in their area and what to use for various ailments. Even today some of the common remedies used by the medical profession are plant based, such as aspirin coming from the bark of a tree and painkillers from the opium poppy. In the household kitchen garlic is said to be one of nature's anti-bacterial agents and ginger is beneficial for aiding circulation.

It became obvious to me that as the human body evolved it obtained all the nutrition it needed from the food available in the natural environment at the time. Try to imagine the stomach as a big bag holding food particles, and the digestive system takes what it can and passes the rest out through the bowels. Now imagine what the mixture in the stomach would have been fifty thousand years ago – it would have conformed to the diet recommendations listed above. Fast forward to the present time and think about what you put in your stomach on a daily basis. Chances are it is nothing much like we evolved on, so if we lack many of the basic nutrients that we evolved on, is it any wonder that our systems are becoming sick.

In the year 2,000 AD I was learning that most diseases of humans were caused by incorrect lifestyle choices. There was not some miracle cure I could learn and then dispense my knowledge to help heal the masses. It was common knowledge in natural therapy circles that lifestyle was the killer. But I noticed at the time medical researchers and scientists were still trying to find drugs that could cure heart disease, cancer, diabetes and obesity, as well as many other diseases. Fifteen years later there has been improvement in the way doctors treat ailments like heart disease and cancer, but most of these improvements have come from early detection and increases in the sophistication of operating procedures, which is still treating the symptoms and not the cause.

However the weight of research evidence is becoming overwhelming in pointing to poor nutrition as being the cause of most disease. The following are some examples of this trend.

Latest Death Stats Highlight Killer Habits (What a wonderful headline to include in this book that discusses the fatal flaw).

Dementia and Alzheimer's disease are taking an increasing toll on Australians, according to the latest Bureau of Statistics cause of death figures. But bad habits are possibly the biggest killer, with close to six out of ten deaths in Australia caused by cancers and cardiovascular disease. They have similar risk factors, noted the Heart Foundation's Dr Rob Grenfell, who called for a co-ordinated approach to smoking, poor nutrition, obesity and physical inactivity.

Another good headline for this book – 'Fruit and Veg Keep the Undertaker Away'.

Eating fruit and veg every day keeps the undertaker at bay. That's the finding of a study that assessed the lifestyle of 65,000 UK adults and compared the eating habits of those who died. Any amount of fruit and vegetables reduces the risk of death, but seven or more servings a day are particularly good, according to the study published in the Journal of Epidemiology and Community Health.

Vegetables offer almost double the benefit of fruit, which shows the Australian guidelines of two fruits and five serves of vegetables a day are spot on. However, only around five per cent of Australian adults meet the target, according to the latest information from the Bureau of Statistics.

The article also says that eating at least seven daily portions was linked to a 42 per cent lower risk of death from all causes.

The following article suggests that looking to modern technology to fix disease may be a forlorn hope.

Article. *"One of Australia's most respected medical specialists has raised the alarm about hyped-up promises of genetic cures for cancers and other diseases. The hype has the potential to do more harm than good, says Dr Robyn Ward, director of cancer services at Sydney's Prince of Wales Hospital, and Professor of Medicines at the University of NSW.*

People with serious illnesses are reading and being told on TV that their genetic information is going to revolutionise their care. However the last time cancer treatment was truly transformed was in the late 1990's with the leukaemia drug Glivec. A decade of promises about personalised cancer medicine has not come to fruition, says Prof Ward, in an editorial in the latest issue of the Medical Journal of Australia."

And here is another article that fully supports what my natural therapies course was teaching me nearly twenty years ago.

Article Headline. The diet that could beat dementia.

The Mediterranean diet could hold the key to beating dementia, the UK's leading physicians have suggested. The diet, which focuses on fresh fruit and vegetables, nuts, fish and olive oil, is possibly the best strategy currently available for preventing Alzheimer's and other conditions involving memory loss, the doctors said. In an open letter to the UK government, the experts urged the medical profession to focus on the benefits of the diet and not on the many dubious drugs flooding the market. The letter's signatories insist numerous studies have proved improvements to lifestyle have a far greater effect in the fight against dementia than anything else, including medications.

"The evidence base for the Mediterranean diet in preventing all of the chronic diseases plaguing the western world is overwhelming" cardiologist Dr Aseem Malhotra says. *"This includes cardiovascular disease, type 2 diabetes, Alzheimer's and cancer."*

"Policy makers and the public need to know that such a diet is far more potent than the often dubious benefit of many medications and without the side effects".

Natural therapists have known this for decades and probably centuries! It was Hippocrates (circa 400 BC) that said *"Let food be thy medicine and let medicine be thy food."*

Exercise (pillar number three)

The human body was designed to move. Just as millions of years of evolution shaped our brains around the ability to love, and our bodies were built from the food we found in the natural environment, exercise, or the necessity for movement within the environment, was also built into our evolutionary process. Back in our hunter/gatherer days exercise was a natural part of our everyday activity. The whole tribe was involved in going out into the landscape, walking many kilometres every day, plus climbing trees for nuts and fruit, and digging for roots and tubers. Exuberant children would be running around all day playing and exploring their environment. Compare that to the present day when most of us take our cars to the supermarket and fill the carts with processed food and sugary drinks. Our culture has also produced many jobs that need brain activity, but very little in the way of physical exercise.

The fact that we do not exercise as much as our bodies have been designed for leads to many health problems, and lack of exercise is a large factor in many early deaths. While researchers tell us exercise can be a beneficial part of effective treatment plans, what is not so well known is the effect exercise has on maintaining a healthy body. Instead of seeing exercise in terms of managing a disease, we should be viewing it as a way of helping to prevent disease in the first place.

Bone strength

When a muscle contracts it puts pressure on the bone where the muscle tendons attach. Repeated exercise (contractions) will cause the body to increase the calcium deposits in the bone to make it stronger. Apparently the biggest factor in having and maintaining good bone density is the amount of exercise a person does. Calcium supplements are often prescribed for those with low bone density, but taking supplements without doing any exercise will not give the best results, as the calcium will not be deposited if it is not needed. I learnt in natural therapy classes that eating calcium rich foods such as nuts and green leafy vegetables, plus regular exercise is the best way to achieve healthy bones.

Oxygenation of the cells

One of the purposes of the blood is to carry oxygen from the lungs to the cells, where it is used to convert carbohydrate to energy. We are all familiar with the larger blood vessels through which blood can flow quite freely. But at the cellular level the blood vessels, known as capillaries, become so narrow that only one haemoglobin (blood) cell at a time can pass through. When we exercise the heart rate and blood pressure builds up, helping to push the blood through the narrow capillaries. Low exercising levels mean that the cells are not getting all the oxygen and other nutrients they need for optimum performance.

Lymph

The lymph system is very rarely mentioned in any discussion about disease states, and I also knew nothing much about this system before my studies. This system has vessels similar to blood vessels. The lymph system acts as 'housecleaner' in that it cleans up the debris from cellular activity. The body produces about 20 litres of interstitial fluid a day, most of which is returned via the blood to the liver and kidneys for processing. Useable products are recycled and waste is eliminated through the urine and faeces. About 3 litres of this interstitial fluid is taken up by the lymph system.

In the lymph nodes lymphocytes deal with any pathogens such as bacteria and any virus that may be trying to establish itself. The lymphocytes also remove any cancer cells that may have originated from a primary cancer elsewhere in the body (ie. a metastasis). Eventually the lymph is deposited back into the larger blood vessels of the upper chest, where it also finds its way to the liver and kidneys for processing.

One important aspect of the lymph system is that it does not have an inbuilt pump, like the heart does for the blood. Instead it relies on muscle movement and pressure gradients to move through the system. Pressure gradients are produced in the chest and stomach cavities as we breathe in and out. Muscle contractions also push the lymph, and this means the movement of lymph relies heavily on exercise. A stagnant lymph flow may increase the chances of cancer forming at the lymph nodes. These cancers are called lymphomas.

General benefits

People who do regular physical exercise have healthier brains and reduce their risk of Alzheimers' disease, according to a paper released to mark the dementia awareness week. *"Apart from overall health benefits, physical activity significantly improves brain health"*, says Dr Maree Fanow, co-author of the paper released by Alzheimers Australia and Fitness Aust. *"About half of Alzheimers disease cases are potentially attributable to risk factors you can change"*, says Dr Fanow. Dr Fanow also states that it is normal for the brain to shrink a little in old age, but this is reduced in people who do regular physical exercise. She also adds that being fit and healthy does matter.

There was a feature on the benefits of exercise in the health and medicine section of The West Australian newspaper, December 28th, 2011. One of the articles claimed that *"....with high blood pressure, heart attack and stroke, probably 80 percent of the risk could be avoided if people kept slim, kept physically active and had a diet that was rich in fruit and vegetables"*(from a Professor Beilin). The same professor also said that if this (exercise) was a drug, it would be regarded as a wonder pill.

Why don't we change ?

All around the world health systems are buckling under the strain of so many sick people, and yet we know from research that probably 80 percent of the load could be reduced by lifestyle changes. Imagine that.... 80 percent of hospital beds closed down because the population is more loving, they get regular exercise and eat their five veg and two fruits on a daily basis. That may mean 80 percent less sick people and then consider the dollars saved by governments on health budgets that could be spent on social and infrastructure programmes.

The natural therapy community understood the importance of life style choices decades ago, and the sheer weight of research evidence is slowly having an effect on scientists and lay people alike. I say slowly because as I was writing this chapter during February 2015, I saw an advertisement on television to raise money for cancer research. 'My goodness', I thought to myself, 'don't they realise that if people changed lifestyle choices up to 80 percent of cancers may not occur.'

Two questions can then be asked. Why do we lifestyle ourselves to early deaths by making bad choices, and why is it so hard to make changes that will drastically improve our overall health? I am going to attempt to answer these two questions.

- Doctors do not learn about the importance of good nutrition and regular exercise. The main focus of their training is on the array of chemicals and surgical procedures that are available to treat symptoms of disease. For example if you go to the doctor and are diagnosed with high blood pressure you are more likely to come home with a packet of chemicals, rather than a box of fruit and vegetables and an exercise programme. In writing this I understand doctors are people who have feelings too, and they all do their best by their patients with the knowledge they have. I see them as being caught up in a health system that has evolved from a material understanding (third level of consciousness) when most of our problems stem from a traumatised brainstem (first level of consciousness).

- Food is too easy to buy off the shelves. It no longer requires hours of toil in a field or chasing game across the plains. Processed food that is calorie rich and nutrient poor dominates many diets, while added flavours, colouring and preservatives provide substances that we did not evolve on. Think of what we are putting in our nutrient bags (stomachs) and then expecting our bodies not to get sick!

- Advertising – we learn from imitation and what's going on in our environment, and the food advertising industry is dominated by food and beverages that are unhealthy. Advertising is mostly misleading and is more concerned about sales than peoples' personal health. We all need to be more educated about the food we eat. Leaving it to people who make money from selling junk food and drink is not a wise thing for our society to do. Studying natural therapies, and specifically herbal medicine and nutrition, was one of the best decisions of my life. It was the antidote I needed against the effects of the advertising industry and living within a culture that seems hell bent on eating itself to death. I believe that a truly loving society will self regulate itself, so all advertising and supermarket shelves will be all about healthy choices. I don't expect to see that in my lifetime, although there are signs attitudes are changing.

- Scientists and researchers are still trying to find ways of treating unhealthy people, and there are many people in the general community who believe that is the way of the future. They believe that the wonder of medical science plus genetic engineering will solve all of humanity's health problems. This is despite the fact that research is showing unequivocally that lifestyle is the cause, so why are some people waiting for medical science to fix any problems when they could be eating good food and jogging around the local park? For any medical cure to be successful it must usually fix the cause, so if the cause is lifestyle how will a tablet fix that? I am not saying it is impossible but from my understanding of science it is highly unlikely.

From my perspective the sleeping giant in influencing our lifestyle choices (the cause) is the force of the imprint from the first level of consciousness. When we carry primal pain we use many ways to keep the pain unconscious, and addictions to food are one of those ways. My own food and drink addictions were ice-cream, alcohol and coffee, plus generally overeating which produced a sluggish body that had trouble feeling anything. I could never let myself get really hungry otherwise I would get agitated. I did not realise the extent of my problem until I addressed the underlying feelings during primal therapy. Ice-cream for me came to represent the comfort I didn't get from my mother, and eating during my infant days was perhaps the only time I got to feel good, so I continued to eat too much as I got older. Now that most of my primal pain has been felt and released I can allow myself to get hungry, and then make good food choices because my body reacts better to good food. Exercise is a priority in my life, and research shows that the best exercise is walking, with some jogging or running to put extra pressure on the system – which is how we evolved.

To treat the cause of our lifestyle dilemma, we need to address the primal pain on the first level of consciousness so that love can rule our life.

In my opinion....

A loving businessman would not build a factory that produced highly processed and sugary foods.

Loving workers would not work in such places.

Loving parents would not feed such food to their children.

Loving people treat their bodies as sacred temples.

A loving society will make sure everyone is included, so that no-one feels lonely, unwanted and useless.

THE NATURE OF LOVE

L ove, love, love. How many songs of all genres and ages contain a powerful reference either directly or indirectly to love. Without doing in-depth research I would say around 60 percent would be a conservative figure. I have some favourite love songs of my own and considering their general popularity, they are obviously the favourites of many other people as well. Johnny Cash and Ring of Fire is one from my era.

The taste of love is sweet
When hearts like ours meet
I fell for you like a child
Ohhh but the fire went wild

The Irish band U2 do not mention love directly within the lyrics of their song, but the reference to fire and the strength of the vocals suggest love was the thing they hadn't found.

I have climbed the highest mountain
I have run through the fields
But I still haven't found what I'm looking for.

I would suggest this particular song was and still is very popular because it resonates so strongly and emotionally with people who still haven't experienced the nature of love in their lives. It was certainly the case for me. Another song I used to sing often was a type of prayer or request to the Universe. The band Foreigner sings,

I want to know what love is
I want you to show me.

Women also sing of love in soft or powerful ways. Bonnie Tyler sings 'Total Eclipse of the Heart' and here is what was said by a reviewer;

"Tyler's powerful vocals are perfectly matched to the song, which

contemplates the trials of love with melodrama and fiery passion."

Jennifer Rush and Celine Dion have both had success with their versions of the passionate song 'The Power of Love', while Whitney Houston had a huge hit with 'I Will Always Love You.'

And then there are the multitude of books and movies that have love and romance as their central theme, with 'chick flicks' (movies) and romantic fiction (books) trying to fill the void within each of us. They touch us for a fleeting moment in time, or maybe stop the void from aching so much while we attach ourselves to hope. Then we may cry a tear from our inner pain, and next day walk around singing,

And I still haven't found what I'm looking for.
But our understanding of love is usually seen and felt through the fog of each individual's level of primal pain and neuroticism, clouding our judgement of what love is and what it is not. Most importantly the repression of primal pain also means that most of the human race cannot feel love at its deepest level, even if they wanted to.

My childhood was spent in a household that had very little love in it, but was made bearable because I had plenty of siblings to have some level of fun with. However I needed to keep myself repressed because it was easy to raise the ire of my father, who seemed to find excuses to punish us when we least expected it. We learnt to keep our natural childhood exuberance under control. Our love of life was replaced with the fear of an angry father and a mother who was too busy to give us the individual attention we all craved.

I married at a young age, and although the relationship seemed to work well for the most part, I always felt a sort of emptiness inside, like something was missing. After thirty years I left the marriage and went to study Natural Therapies in the hope of being able to heal my psychological problems.

My main passion though, was to find out what love was. I read lots of books about relationships and other aspects of love, and it became obvious to me that love was the thing missing from my life, and that lack of love was responsible for the emptiness I felt inside me. However none of the books I had read could tell me how to find love, what it was, how I would recognise it if I found it, or how to live a more loving life. At the same time I was suffering very low self esteem and suicidal depression. No professional person could tell me what my brain was doing, and least of all, how I could stop it from behaving in uncontrollable ways.

Eventually I went to America to undergo primal therapy for my psychological problems, and to my relief the therapy was very successful. I learnt about and experienced the three levels of consciousness and how my first level stored enormous quantities of primal pain, the second level was awash in negative and horrible feelings, which caused my third level to become dysfunctional. What a revelation, at last I understood my problem. The bad news was that reliving the trauma was the only way to heal, and even in small doses, was a very painful and relentless experience.

However, much to my surprise, as the pain left my body I started to *feel* my body and my life. At first I started to feel good feelings that I had never felt previously, the feelings then intensified until I started feeling what I believe to be love. From my understanding of the human brain my sensation of love would have been facilitated by a flow of oxytocin. This was a truly profound experience, because I had been reading so many articles and books on love trying to understand what it was. Now I knew it was not something to be learned intellectually, it was something that had to be experienced. Love was a sensation that had the power to overwhelm all other thoughts and feelings.

Using my proposed GAL score with self assessment (introduced in an earlier chapter) undergoing primal therapy raised my GAL score from 50 to 85. This shift provided a tremendous contrast between what my feeling life was before therapy, and what it is now. Not many people in this world have these points of reference, so they have no idea of what is possible in life. An added benefit is that I now have the resources to release my primal pain when it is triggered, rather than project it onto others, or suppress it. This ability means my life has the capacity to get better and better as I keep releasing my primal pain.

In contrast I believe the general population have static GAL scores, because they do not understand the three levels of consciousness and the inbuilt fatal flaw in order to do anything meaningful about it. The only way to raise a GAL score is to feel the primal pain stored on the first level of consciousness, and our culture has no widespread understanding of how to do that, or even that it exists. The cognitive type therapies, medication and psychoanalytical approaches that dominate the mental health field deal only in symptom management at the third level of consciousness. Good primal therapy opens up a person's second level of consciousness (the feelings) before taking them deeper into their first level of consciousness (sensations) where they get to deal with painful imprinting. Ridding the body/mind of painful imprinting allows feelings of love to flow more freely.

After my experience of reading many books about love and then finally being able to *feel* love, I consider myself to have a slightly better than average understanding in matters of love. From this position I will share my understanding of what love is and what it isn't. As far as I know love is not a subject that is studied in any university anywhere in the world.

The sensation/feeling of love gives a person a certain nature, or way of behaving in this world. For example a person with a GAL score of 45 will have a very different nature than a person with a score of 90. It also needs to be understood that it is primarily a person's early environment that determines their GAL score, and not their genetic inheritance. Before I explain what the nature of love is as I have experienced it, I will give an overview of the known physical pathways of love within the human brain .

The physical pathways of love in the brain

There is a physical pathway in the brain known as the pleasure pathway. It starts in the ventral tegmentum area (top of the brainstem) and radiates to the nucleus accumbens and other limbic system structures, before going upward and forward into the prefrontal cortex. Note that this pathway involves all three levels of consciousness. The main neurotransmitter in this pathway is dopamine, so when we feel a rush of pleasure it is facilitated by a flow of dopamine.

Professor Pfaus from the Concordia University in Montreal, Canada, says that pleasure is experienced when we eat good food or have sex, and then love comes out of that ,which is represented in another brain area *"Love is actually a habit that is formed from sexual desire as desire is rewarded"* Prof Pfaus says. The important thing to understand about love is that it is an addiction. *"It works the same way in the brain as when people are addicted to drugs"* Prof Pfaus adds.

Comment.   Many addiction studies are focused on the dopamine pathway, but primal theory says dopamine is the messenger acting on the second level of consciousness, while the message is being instigated on the first level. Artificially changing levels of dopamine is not going to alter the underlying problem.

Prof Pfaus also says *"Love was not necessarily a bad habit, activating many brain pathways involved in bonding and monogamy."*

My argument would be that love is a primal force that facilitates the primal need for pair bonding and monogamy, which forms the basis of our successful evolution. Oxytocin and prolactin are two hormones that facilitate our feelings of love, and in my experience that does not happen until our GAL score reaches 80 or above. Primal theory, as I understand it, says that each person's number one need in life is to be loved, and research in brain architecture supports that theory. When we don't get love early in life, a love that fires up and moulds our developing brains, we will adopt other ways to achieve pleasurable states of mind, hence addictions of all types are rife in the human species.

Without going into complex detail, pain and pleasure share the same pathways, so when a child suppresses overwhelming pain, that same action also suppresses the ability to feel good feelings, such as love. For example depression is known for its low joy of life.

The insula, which lies close to the limbic system, is known to modulate the pain response, and serotonin receptors between the left and right prefrontal cortex may also be part of the pain modulation pathway. Brain scientists understand this from a physical perspective, such as the pain from a burn or a broken leg. However we also have psychological pain pathways from primal pain, and these pathways may be the same, the brain not being able to distinguish between the two. I assert throughout this book that when scientists understand the three levels of consciousness, they will be able to interpret their brain research in a vastly different way.

If I put a primal theory perspective on another of Prof Pfaus' statements, I can feel sexual pleasure at a lower level which provides the impetus for intercourse (dopamine) but not at a high enough level to feel love (oxytocin). This is an important aspect of human functioning, and the reason why we can reproduce, without going deep enough into feelings to facilitate pair bonding and monogamy. We only need to look at the number of single parent families to see the results of that part of our brain functioning – or dysfunction.

Prof Pfaus also says *"But much of what made love a many splendid thing remained a mystery to science."*

Comment.   That mystery will remain until science understands there are three levels of consciousness, and that the three levels create different states of mind, have different ways of speaking to us, and have differing intelligences. The first level is very intelligent in its own way, and also exerts the most influence on how we live our life. It is also the level at which the power of love originates.

The nature of love - or - how a loving person acts

My understanding of the nature of love is that it starts life as a sensation in the lower brain that is transformed into a feeling in the limbic system that is experienced by the prefrontal cortex. Sensations and feelings can never be described in writing in a way that even comes close to explaining what they are. As I will repeat very often in this book, sensations and feelings have to be experienced. However a person who has a GAL score of 90+ will express themselves in this world in a very different way to somebody else with a score of 45. I will use electricity and light as a useful analogy.

For example a 12 volt battery driven torch can give a useful light, but the 240 voltage power of households (in Australia) can give a much brighter light. A person with a GAL score of 45 will only express love at the level of a 12 volt illumination. At this power the strength of love is weak, and as a consequence the person can do plenty of unloving things, such as domestic violence, rape, taking drugs to try to increase their brightness, being cruel to animals and controlling others. Depression, anxiety and other mental disorders also flourish in the poor light.

A person with a GAL score of 90 or more is equivalent to a powerful 240 volt light at high watts. The power of the light (love) is so strong that the person cannot deviate from its field of illumination. At this level love goes from being experienced as esoteric in nature, to having its own energetic field that drives a person to do the right thing by his fellow man. The following pages will attempt to illustrate how a loving person will talk and behave, with the emphasis on the fact that talking and behaviour are not love themselves, but are products of loves 'light'.

Calmness and Confidence - The loving person has a calmness and confidence that comes from a sense of self – of high self esteem; a feeling of being wanted and loved for who they are – something that the parents imprinted into the childs brainstem early in life. A lot of pregnancies are unwanted, and so the baby comes into this world and quickly senses that it is just a nuisance. Even if babies are planned and wanted, our culture and belief systems generally do not provide for the early needs of children. The materialistic society we have created restricts the ability to satisfy childhood needs of loving human interactions that develop a strong social brain. It is the brain that will determine how a person experiences their life; whether a person is mostly calm and confident or whether they are stressed and have low self esteem.

Sacredness and Altruism - The loving person feels their own lives are sacred, and therefore everyone else's life is too. It is an honour and privilege to be on this earth and experience the beauty of just being alive. Most of the old religious texts discuss this aspect of being human, and extend it to all living things as well as to the earth we live on. The idealism contained in the principles of Buddhism is such an example.

We all tend to *think* about love because that is what we are taught. Thinking only produces ideas that have no inherent loving power, because they are only 'thoughts'. Love contains within it the ideals of sacredness and altruism, so when we are expressing love our thoughts and actions will demonstrate these qualities in an automatic and forceful way. (The brain also works this way in panic attacks. A terror filled brainstem will create panic attacks automatically and forcefully).

Human relationships are a much researched area in psychology and specifically many groups of researchers have tried to identify the qualities needed for a good marraige. One such group of researchers (unnamed) came up with seven qualities, which were positivity, understanding, giving assurance, self disclosure, openness, sharing tasks and involving their partner's family and friends. All these things could be described as love in action, meaning if a person has a positively imprinted (loved) brainstem then these actions will be automatic and forceful. A loving person will naturally behave in the above ways. If a person had a traumatic childhood they would tend to struggle in a marriage because they do not have good relationship imprinting. They may be able to learn about good qualities and try to change their behaviour, but it is a real struggle to try and overcome the original imprinting.

Beliefs - The loving person will have very few dogmatic beliefs. Religious and political beliefs are the cause of much human suffering, and have their origin in early traumatic environments. Our painful pasts, imprinted in the brainstem, drive our beliefs because beliefs are part of the human brains defence system that keeps primal pain from surfacing. As the disconnection between our pain and reality becomes larger, we lose touch with feelings altogether, and that's when we can and do cause harm to each other. People who have undergone primal therapy understand this because the therapy gets them in contact with their own imprinted pain.

A loving person has strong contact with their feelings, and when they are feeling on the second level, it is difficult to hold onto any belief systems. As the person descends into pure sensation it is impossible to have belief systems at all, because they are experiencing a completely different way of being in this world. So one may ask the question – when the person returns to their third level won't the previously held belief system still be there? My answer is that experiencing the first level of consciousness directly will change a persons' reality on the third level (discussed more fully in the next two chapters). All religious, political and other beliefs disappear at the first level of consciousness. This phenomenon of the human mind is not widely understood. In fact all thinking ceases when we experience the sensation of love in its purest form. That is why love is so important as a state of mind. In this state all things are sacred and so deliberately hurting others is not possible. Our genetic history must have evolved this way and love embedded in our DNA is the force that has driven our success as a species on this planet. We don't need religion or politics to dictate a moral code; we already have a very effective inbuilt moral code. Disconnection from this loving force is part of our fatal flaw. Religion, politics and most other strong belief systems are a substitute for all those who are disconnected from true love.

Health - A loving person will be physically and mentally very healthy. Love does not contain any addictions, apart from the scientific view that love itself is an addiction, and behaves like one. The nature of an addiction (and love) is that a person needs their fix every day, that they will do strange things to attain that fix, and will not rest until they get their fix. When the addictive force of love is not in our bodies, that same force will drive people to find a substitute, which so often means putting things in our bodies that cause ill health.

Most importantly loving people will generally not be living a fast-paced life that is full of stress, because stress is a third level reaction to perceived threats, many of which originate from painful imprints. Stress produces cortisol which is a known risk factor in many physical and mental diseases. Loving people will bring other loving persons into their lives, and through being more socially connected also lowering the risk factors of succumbing to disease states.

Inner Beauty – a loving person does not necessarily have to be extremely physically beautiful or handsome, because the inner beauty is the most important part of being with another. Loving people do not have the annoying neurotic behaviours or addictions that destroy so many relationships. They are usually pleasant people to be around. Thomas Jefferson, an American President, said it like this, "*I see now our fireside formed into a groupe, no one member of which has a fibre in their composition which can ever produce any jarring or jealousies among us. No irregular passions, no dangerous bias, which may render problematical the future fortunes and happiness of our descendants.*" Thomas Jefferson may have said this in a different context to what this book is about, but the quote is none-the-less relevant for this book.

Our present culture places a lot of emphasis on physical beauty. The craziness of the modelling world leaves a lot of young adults, especially girls, feeling less than adequate. The beauty industry is capitalising on this obsession with physical beauty, with parlours that cater for the latest trends in makeup and manicures springing up everywhere. From my male perspective a woman expressing her full loving nature is by far the most powerful aphrodisiac I have ever experienced.

Bullies and Criticism – The natural action of a loving person is to respect other peoples' feelings. A bully is usually a person who feels weak inside, probably because they have been stripped of their own power by abusing, over critical or neglectful parents. They can regain some power in their lives by picking on others weaker than themselves. Bullies will quite often gather supporters from those who have very little internal power of their own, and therefore seek it in being a member of a strong gang. This happens at all levels in our society, becoming obvious in schoolyards and then progressing to teenage gangs who rule some neighbourhoods. At the adult level there are drug dealing gangs and some bikie gangs that have little regard for law and order. We even have governments of whole countries who bully their citizens into submission at the point of a gun. Timid low self esteem people will let themselves be bullied and criticized (the proverbial doormat), mainly because they endured similar behaviour from parents. A loving person is not a natural bully and also knows that criticism is harmful, especially to a developing brain.

Toughness - From a man's point of view love has given me an inner strength. 'Toughen up sunshine' and 'real men don't cry' are unfortunate phrases that reflect our cultures view of what it means to be a man. For any human, not crying when we need to is not toughness, it is not listening to, or not feeling, what our body needs. Our culture too often sees crying as a weakness, especially in men. With crying also comes the fear of 'falling apart', or 'losing it'.

Being tough by not crying is detrimental to our long term health. Anything repressed also represses other physiological responses in our mind and body, and so we run the risk of becoming emotionally and physically sick. I know this because primal therapy for me was, and still is, mostly about crying the tears I did not cry as a child. Doing so has lifted the repression that had ruined much of my life.

Love gives a man the strength to provide safety for his family, but also the *softness* and *gentleness* that his partner and children need. The ability to cry is an important part of being a healthy and loving human, and gives a man true toughness. In fact every male or female of any age needs to cry when their inner psyche has been hurt. The way to mend the hurt is to feel it and cry it out. It is part of our human make-up.

The current rise in post-traumatic stress disorder is happening because our culture does not fully understand what effects traumatic experiences have on the first level of consciousness, and even less how to deal with them.

Happiness – A loving person will be naturally happy, and happy people are good to be around. They are happy with the way their lives are and enjoy being in this world. There are many people researching happiness and others write books on how to be happy, but happiness is the product of a person in love with life. Trying to make someone happy by altering their behaviour at the third level of consciousness is a mighty task, because these people generally have traumatic imprinting that makes them feel sad and unhappy, therefore negative thoughts will naturally dominate.

A human cannot express pure love and happiness while they carry any primal pain. Primal pain denies access to love and therefore the happiness that comes from being in love with one's life.

Raising Children - Understanding the nature of love is so important when it comes to raising children. A person with a GAL score of 90+ will radiate a loving persona, aura or energy field. At birth the baby has an active brainstem that contains his sensing apparatus, so a baby can sense whether an action or energy is loving or unloving. It does not understand belief systems of any kind because these are all third level activities, and the young baby is not born with a functioning third level of consciousness. In fact imposing these things on a baby and infant will cause stress on the developing brain. In my own journey to find love, I have met many people who were raised in religious families who are in the same struggle, their parents mistaking religious dogma for love. For a baby to achieve a GAL score of 90+ it needs to be surrounded by people with similar scores.

Attachment Theory is based on a well researched psychological understanding that the early years of a child's development depend a lot on the way babies attach to their mothers. Research has shown that a parent changing their behaviour in child rearing can produce better attachment outcomes, but this approach does not explain the power of an aura or energy field generated from the consequent sensations which affect the baby's brain. If a parent has a low GAL score they will have a corresponding low 'quality of love' aura for the baby to read. The fact someone understands Attachment Theory and practices parenting accordingly does not necessarily mean a healthily attached child. Learning Attachment Theory, or any other child rearing process, is a third level intellectual activity, but it needs to be delivered from the first level of sensations and the second level of feeling, because these are the levels that the infant is communicating at.

For example many people are depressed or fearful, and these conditions are difficult to hide from a baby; you can't fool a baby's sensing brain. There is a lot of research showing that people with psychological disorders have a lot higher risk of their offspring developing disorders. The Adverse Childhood Experience (ACE) research is one such focus that is gaining a lot of attention at the moment.

However, changing a parenting technique does lead to some level of improvement, both in the outcome for the child, and also in enhancing family dynamics. After one of my clients started experiencing the 'awfulness' of his own upbringing during therapy, he was able to use this knowledge to calm the friction within the family unit, spend more quality time with his children, and understand that a good life is about experiencing love, and very little to do with pursuing materialism.

Anyone can feel the effect of other people's auras'. We all know that it is better to be around happy people than depressed people, and it is better to have friends who either give praise, or accept us for who we are, rather than those who constantly criticize. I am well into my seventh decade of life and the current paradigm suggests at this age I should be unaffected by the actions of others. However I am still amazed at how different people will affect me in different ways. I do not choose my feelings. They happen automatically and come from my sensing apparatus. In fact since I have undergone primal therapy, and am therefore more in touch with my feelings, I am aware of how strongly other peoples' auras' will affect my own feelings.

(For good descriptions of the way human brains are sculptured by other human brains, read "A General Theory of Love" by Lewis, Amini and Lannon, and also "The Neuroscience of Human Relationships – Attachment and the Developing Social Brain" by Louis Cozolino).

The power of love – or the love of power

There are some well known phrases that try to capture the nature of love, such as 'When you have love you have everything', 'Love is all there is', and 'Love is all you need'. Another that is so important for our times is 'we either have the power of love, or if not we substitute it with the love of power'. The problem with talking about love is that it is just rhetoric and rhetoric about love does not have the same effect as actually feeling love. An intellectual knowledge of some of the aspects of love will not change deep-seated behaviour.

From the three levels of consciousness, it can be understood that if we have love imprinted on the first level then we will automatically be expressing love in our actions and thinking on the third level, and that is all we need to live a wonderful and meaningful life. Of course we also need food, water, shelter and exercise, but these things will flow naturally from a caring community and abundant nature. If we do not have love on the first level, then the third level of consciousness will be dominated by our need to obtain substitutes. Obtaining these substitutes quite often means we have to exert power and control over others, we gather physical wealth regardless of the plight of other people and all living things, and we are so driven by it that we are capable of destroying the very environment that sustains us.

Despite the lack of love on this earth there are still many people trying to do the right thing. Our inbuilt altruistic nature is a powerful force. However the driving demand to meet our neurotic needs is also a powerful force. Corruption of all kinds, and at all levels of society, from individuals to companies and governments, provides a hefty barrier to the sharing of assets and commodities that would provide the necessities of life to every human.

A loving person is not corruptible because they already have more than they need, such is the power of love. In my experience love has a law that states 'don't take what is not yours, and don't take more than you need.' But the world still has many individuals, and companies who are run by individuals, accruing vast wealth way beyond what they need to survive, or even to live a very comfortable life.

What these people are doing is trying to obtain enough material things to compensate for the big black void in them where love should have been imprinted. I could say a painful and scary big black void, because during my therapy I stood on the edge of that black void many times while trying to gain the courage to jump into the darkness where I knew extreme pain lurked.

At this time I will deviate slightly to explain a widely misunderstood part of the human psyche. There are those who believe that parts of a persons' subconscious mind are so dark and horrible that the memories should never be relived or dealt with in therapy. I have personally known of some people who have reached these dark places in various types of therapy and have been told by the therapist to go no further. The internet advertises and discusses many different types of healing modalities, and among these are those that say it is not necessary to dig up the horrors of the past. Other therapists have tried to open people into these places, with disastrous outcomes because they haven't experienced their own dark places and/or haven't been trained in the correct procedures. Primal therapy takes a person to these dark and painful places in a controlled way, in the knowledge that true healing can only occur when these 'dark forces', or primal pain leave the body.

Experiencing primal pain also informs a person of how deeply a human brain can be traumatised if it is not loved early in life. Ignoring these dark places or trying to skip around them does very little in advancing our understanding of how the brain functions. I believe if we are to survive as a species it will be necessary to understand these dark places, what causes them, and then try to eliminate them because their presence ruins so many lives.

Another aspect of not dealing with primal pain is that affected people will not get to experience the full power of love while on this planet, and that is a real shame. There is good and bad in almost every person's basement, and the 'good' (love) cannot be felt until the 'bad' (pain) is dissipated.

Three levels of consciousness and human behaviour

There is a big advantage in understanding the triune brain as having different levels of consciousness, especially in how these levels interact in influencing human behaviour. The lower brain provides for our humanness, which encompasses love and gives life its meaning.

As a contrast the third level deals in the world of ideas, beliefs, material possessions and money – the 'wants' of life. None of these third level creations are essential for life. Understanding this situation means we know that if we lose all the 'out there' things, such as a job, savings and beliefs, then we still have the most important part – we still have ourselves, meaning we can still experience love; the most important thing in a human life.

The Wall Street financial area in New York is one place where the human race shows its hunger for wealth, evidenced by greed and corruption. I don't particularly understand the capitalist money system at this level, although I suppose it has some positive function. However an enduring picture I have of Wall Street is that when things are good, people can make incredible amounts of money. From my Australian perspective the most venerated men in the USA are the ones who can make megabucks on Wall Street. The other picture I have is that when things go bad and people lose money they stand on window ledges and step into oblivion. What they are implying by jumping from buildings is that money is representing all levels of the 'self', and if they have money then they feel like a successful human. If they suddenly lose all their money that means to them that they are not successful as a human, and that feeling will drive them to suicide. They don't understand that life is mainly about the first and second levels of consciousness, and these levels don't deal in material assets such as money, and can't be taken away.

The loving person is not reliant on third level activities for their sense of self. Their only real need is to love and be loved, which when experienced in its full power is more than enough.

Our current economic systems rely on growth of around at least three or four percent annually. There are an increasing number of people who say this can't go on forever because it is using too many of the worlds' finite resources. However governments are loathe to take action because negative growth means recession, and recession usually means loss of government at the next election. Most of us in the western world could afford to live a less materialistic lifestyle, but it is difficult to reduce consumerism and wealth creation when so many people identify their status in life by the material wealth they have. But we should not be afraid of losing everything that has been created with the third level of consciousness, because these are just 'wants'.

Most of the people in the western world could reduce their 'wants' by 3 or 4 percent a year until their collective requirements return to some sort of balance with nature. The good thing is we do not need to have a corresponding reduction in our need for love because there is more than enough actual and latent love in the world to fulfil everyone's need, and it is instantly renewable. Such is the nature of love.

Leo Tolstoy on love

"Love is the only way to rescue humanity from all ills."

"But one thing only is needed : the knowledge of the simple and clear truth which finds place in every soul that is not stupefied by religion and scientific superstition – the truth that for our life one law is valid – the law of love, which brings the highest happiness to every individual as well as to all of mankind."

FALSE BELIEFS

The main premise of the fatal flaw theory in the human brain is that there are three levels of consciousness, and that the flaw occurs because of a major disconnection between the second level (feelings) and the third level (cognition). In a healthy mind all three levels are fully connected, so a loved brainstem will be the driving force of sensations that determine our feelings, and feelings will be experienced and interpreted for what they are in the prefrontal cortex.

If the brainstem imprints were ones of feeling unloved, it is then forced to carry a large pool of primal pain. An unloved brainstem lives in fear of its very life, so the forces generated have a life or death intensity. This explains why sensations in the lower brain have such a powerful destabilising affect higher up in the brain. The painful feelings are very difficult to deal with because of their overpowering awfulness.

With painful feelings always on the rise, and their overwhelming nature threatening survival, the upper part of the brain has to take action to keep the primal pain out of conscious awareness. In psychological terms this is called a defence system, and multiple neurotic behaviours are created as part of this system that keeps primal pain suppressed.

One common way it does this is to create false beliefs, with those beliefs then becoming the person's way of avoiding their primal pain. We know this from primal therapy because when underlying primal pain is felt, belief systems will change or drop away altogether. The therapist does not tell the patient what to believe or how to run their lives – they only help the patient to rid their minds of pain, and then the patient is free to be themselves at last.

Louis Cozolino is a psychotherapist who wrote a book titled *'Healing the Social Brain'* and he describes the defence system thus (p23), *'The neural connections that result in defences shape our lives by selecting what we approach and avoid, what our attention is drawn to, and the assumptions we use to organise our experiences. Our cortex then provides us with rationalization and beliefs about our behaviours that help keep our coping strategies and defences in place, possibly for a lifetime. These neural and psychic structures can lead to either psychological and physical health, or illness and disability.'*

Jean Jensen in her book *Reclaiming Your Life* writes *'The unconscious defences of repression and denial work together to protect human beings from the awareness of truth or experience which could threaten their survival.'* And on page 17, *'Another serious consequence of continued repression has to do with the way in which the unconscious is forced to function in order to maintain it. The sorting-out requires that reality be distorted sufficiently to control the impact of any particular event. In other words, an inborn human capacity – the ability to process experience – is damaged.'* And later – *'What usually happens is that the unconscious distorts perception without the individuals being aware of it.'*

This last point of Jensen's is very important in understanding our fatal flaw. It highlights the fact that the subconscious mind has a powerful intelligence that operates outside the knowledge of the cognitive mind. Most humans think they are rational, unaware that the subconscious is actually making them act irrationally so as to protect them from feeling their primal pain.

This division in the human brain begins in childhood. At first we act from natural impulses that are guided by the way we sense and feel. A newborn baby experiences its life as a sensation, and at six months its limbic, or feeling system, develops more fully. The child only starts to *think* about its environment at around two years of age. So in our early years we are mostly a *sensing/feeling* being, and that's how we deal with our world.

At its core love is a powerful sensation, and a baby can *sense* whether it is loved or not. If a child is expressing itself in a natural way, and parents do not support or react positively, the child becomes confused. The child may learn that 'being myself' is not safe, or mummy or daddy do not love me if I do certain things – 'they do not love me for who I am'. This causes the child to try to become 'somebody else', creating an unreal self in an effort to gain their parents love. In that sense they create a false reality of themselves and the world around them that stays with them for a lifetime.

David McRaney explores this effect in several books he has written, one of which is titled *You are Now Less Dumb*. The following is an extract.

"The last one hundred years of research suggests that you, and everyone else, still believe in a form of naive realism. You still believe that although your inputs may not be perfect, once you get to thinking and feeling, those thoughts and feelings are reliable and predictable. We now know that you can never know how much of subjective reality is a fabrication because you never experience anything other than the output of your mind. Everything that's ever happened to you has happened within your skull."

My own experience is that before primal therapy my mind was terribly confused, and everything that was happening seemed like a jumbled mess. In fact many parts of my mind were doing things that other parts of my mind were labelling irrational. Post primal therapy I now know and experience my mind has having three separate parts, those being the cognitive, the feelings and then sensations, with the brainstem sensations being the most powerful and influential in the way I live my life. I am no longer confused because I know what area each part of my brain is operating in. Before undergoing primal therapy I would have regarded anything lower than my third level as being in my unconscious. But primal therapy brought my lower levels to conscious awareness, and now I regard my sensations and feelings as part of my conscious state. This is proving to be a much better way of being in this world.

The problem with the psychology industry approach is that they see the brains output as a whole, and are unable or unwilling to distinguish its separate parts. This is reflected in their approach to treatments, which are mostly only partially effective because they do not alter the original imprinting, and so don't bring the unconscious to consciousness. It stays repressed by a powerful defence system.

So now I will challenge McRaney's statement that *"We now know that there is no way you can ever know an objective reality."* My own reality, post primal therapy, is a lot more objective than before, mainly because it is based on my conscious sensations and feelings, and not false beliefs. McRaney also writes *"and we now know that you can never know how much of subjective reality is a fabrication."* But McRaney obviously does not understand primal theory and therapy, because this therapy gets under the fabrication, not by dismantling the fabrication, but by bringing up the underlying feeling that caused the fabrication in the first place. Once the feelings and associated pains are felt, the fabrication drops away. The patient then becomes more objective, because he has access to his real self.

In a review of McRaney's book, Maria Popova writes "*In sum we are excellent at deluding ourselves and terrible in recognising when our own perceptions, attitudes, impressions and opinions about the external world are altered from within*" and also "*Self delusion is as much a part of the human condition as fingers and toes*".

An example from my own vast store of delusions was my belief that I was unlovable (my parents did not love me so who would) and women do not like sex (from my parents dysfunctional sex life). This delusional state of mine played itself out in my relationships with women, making my life more miserable than it needed to be. My *subjective* view was not real. I now know that I am lovable and that women do enjoy sex. In fact both these things are important in the continuation of the human species, so evolution has favoured men who are lovable by women, and women who have the capacity to enjoy sex, (provided they have access to their full loving feelings and the sex is not forced on them).

I can say my reality is a lot more objective because I have experienced living with a very subjective brain (for 55 years), and after primal therapy I am experiencing living a life with a brain that is a lot more objective. The person who has a high GAL score, and therefore has access to powerful sensations and feelings, will have an objective reality, and the lower the score, the more subjective that reality becomes.

How the human brain forms a strong subjective (mostly false) reality as it crosses from the second level of feelings into the third level of cognition is one of the keys to understanding the Fatal Flaw.

False beliefs have three components.

Certainty – they are held with absolute conviction.

Incorrigibility – not changeable by compelling counter-argument or proof to the contrary.

Impossibility of falsity of content despite being implausible, bizarre or patently untrue.

People create all sorts of false beliefs, but I will focus on religion because millions of people have died, and millions of people have become murderers of religious believers, all because of false beliefs. Most of the religions of the world are characterised by the above three definitions. Before any religious believers throw this book down I believe that religion is mostly based on faith and false beliefs that are generated by a cortex that is trying to avoid the pain of an unloved childhood. Our true and very powerful spirituality, our altruistic nature, in my experience, is a function of the human brainstem, or our first level of consciousness, which is Godlike in its nature. I will build my case throughout this book.

Core beliefs are generated from our early environment and relationship with other humans, especially our parents. If a person's early childhood was experienced as loving and positive, then the core beliefs generated will lead the person through a happy and loving life. However a traumatic childhood leads to a person developing core beliefs that do not generate an ideal life. The following is a list of common negative core beliefs.

* I am always wrong

* I do not matter

* I am not understood

* I do not fit in anywhere

* I am unattractive

* There is something wrong with me

* I am useless

* No-one loves me

Core beliefs generally have a great deal of truth in them, because this is how a child feels when they are not loved as a baby and infant. There is a lot of primal pain attached to these core beliefs, because the realization that *I am not good enough to be loved* is a devastating experience for a young child. Therefore these beliefs are hidden from conscious awareness but because they are part of an imprint they have a powerful influence on the choices people make through all stages of life. Primal therapy deals with these core beliefs by removing the primal pain contained in early memories.

Believing that something is true does not make it so. Let's look at beliefs from a triune brain perspective. During primal therapy a person starts in his prefrontal cortex (thinking state) and goes down into their feeling state in the limbic system. At the beginning there is a mix of thinking and feeling, but as a person descends further, the feelings start to dominate until the conscious state is almost pure feeling. It is important to understand that this feeling state does not contain any ideas or beliefs – just observation from the conscious observer. (The conscious observer is the part of the cognitive brain that remains aware, at all times, during therapy).

The journey downward continues into the basement where consciousness is experienced as a sensation. The conscious observer is still present, but its influence is minimal. The body may twist and turn in agony, or the voice is only able to produce grunts and groans, and the person realises they are in the grip of their reptilian brain. People who attain this state of mind during therapy know there is another part of the brain that is in control, and that they have found a level of consciousness and intelligence they had no idea existed. Most importantly, in this state of mind, a person will realise they are experiencing the world as it is, and not what they believe it to be. At this level of brain operation there are no belief systems, because the prefrontal cortex is almost completely shut down. When observing a person in this state it looks like they are in a deep trance and experiencing something very primal and very powerful. These are the states of mind that bring the deepest healing because this is where the original painful imprints reside, and where they need to be dealt with.

Reliving the original imprinted memory is powerfully awful – the experience of not having one's early needs met is incredibly mind bending. A lot of patients report that they feel as if they will go insane if they visit those dark places, but it is where they need to go if they want to become healthy. I cannot emphasize enough the awfulness and strength of these feelings, but I need to try because this imprinted pain is the root cause of the fatal flaw. From my hard-won experience in primal therapy it is my opinion that *the strength and influence of the first line of consciousness that resides in the brainstem is grossly misunderstood by all in the psychology industry.*

There is a correlation between the insanity and craziness of these primal feelings, and in the way they are diverted into insane and crazy actions and beliefs that are generated in the cortex of an afflicted person. A crazy and insane person in his third level of consciousness has most likely suffered crazy and insane treatment as a child. As a therapist I listen to these stories of how well intentioned but 'unfeeling' parents have treated their children, sometimes in quite brutal ways. A patient undergoing primal therapy will usually need to express themselves in a crazy and insane way during therapy to get the painful energy out of their system.

From the perspective of having dealt with my own insanity, and now being a therapist for others, I understand the cause of addictions, depression, anxiety, the crazy ideas that abound in many religions, wars, narcissism, racism, and divorces. In my opinion they all have their basis in extreme primal pain at the first level of consciousness.

Fortunately there is another dimension to the power of the brainstem sensations. Just as a primal imprint can be powerfully bad, if the brainstem is allowed to develop in an ideal environment, the resultant imprints can be powerfully good. My first experience of this in myself took me by complete surprise. For some time I was good friends with a female, and one particular day we had a very pleasant time together. As I gave her a hug goodbye, I was overwhelmed by a strange and strong feeling that was a whole-of-body experience. The feeling was so strange and unexpected that it caused me to walk unsteadily to my car, and after driving out of sight I stopped to collect my thoughts. I had spent many years trying to understand what love was from an intellectual level, and that evening, at the age of 62, I believe that what I had just felt was love – for the first time in my life. So that was why I could never cognitively 'figure out' what love was. Love is a feeling, not a thinking, and there is a world of difference between the two.

Several years later I went to an open air cinema with some friends from a social group. I had got to know a particular female, having been on several previous social outings together in the group. This night she was dressed up in a long casual dress that displayed bare shoulders and a teasing cleavage. Before the movie she was relaxed and happy and looked truly elegant as we talked about our recent lives. After the movie I was standing next to her in the group as we discussed the storyline of the movie, when I became overwhelmed with a body sensation that I can only describe as pure beauty. It was like watching a spectacular sunset, only the sensation was a hundred times stronger. It was not the same feeling as the love that I had experienced previously, and it was not sexual in nature, as I perhaps would have expected of myself. Although I had always enjoyed the beauty of the female form, I had never experienced anything as intense as that before. Before primal therapy I would have described what I sensed as being a spiritual experience, but I knew that it must have been my brain sensations letting me experience the beauty standing next to me.

Undergoing primal therapy has exposed me to some of the worst feelings a human can experience, but having done so I can now enjoy some of the best. The benefit of primal therapy is that I have been able to 'exorcise' my painful past that was making my life hell on earth. The most exciting benefit is that I now have access to my good feelings, and they will be readily available to me for the rest of my days. I am able to live much of my life in my feelings, which is a good mind space to be in.

All my negative belief systems have changed or dropped away altogether. Once upon a time I believed that people had choices, and they were obnoxious, took drugs, and broke the law just for the adventure of it. I now know that these people are governed by a disordered first line of consciousness, so although I don't agree with how they act, I believe they really do not have much choice in the matter. They need to feel their pain or act in a way that keeps them from it, so they really do need their belief systems to assist in avoiding their primal pain.

"Our knowledge of neuroscience highlights the fact we primates have complex and imperfect brains and should remain sceptical about what we think we know. In other words primates would be wise to doubt their beliefs and remain open to new ideas." (Louis Cozolino).

My own experience was that when I become more real I developed an expanded consciousness because I was freed from my limited view of life that I had formed and maintained through rigid belief systems.

David Bohms was a theoretical physicist who also contributed innovative and unorthodox ideas to neuropsychology and the philosophy of mind. (Wikipedia). This is one of Bohm's quotes.

*"To keep repeating a baleful (*malicious or harmful*) pattern without recognising that we are caught in its loop is one of life's greatest tragedies; to recognise it but feel helpless in breaking it is one of our greatest trials; to transcend the fear of uncertainty, which undergirds all such patterns of belief and behaviour, is a supreme triumph."*

To underscore the effect that belief systems have we need look no further than what was happening in the Middle East as the year 2015 came to a close. Politics and religion were at the forefront of a malicious and harmful pattern without the many protagonists being aware they were caught in the loop Bohm describes in the first sentence above. Consequently the Middle East was (and as you read this, probably still is) caught up in one of humanity's greatest tragedies.

In the second part of Bohm's statement he suggests that some people understand the loop but are powerless to help. How many people do you, the reader, know who are in a negative loop and you feel powerless to stop them?

In the third step transcending the situation seems almost impossible.

Transcendence can come through accessing love at the first level of human consciousness, but whether we ever get to achieve that ideal at a species level is questionable. It will certainly be one of humanity's *supreme triumphs* if it occurs.

ALTERED MIND STATES

Our culture does not have one single paradigm or understanding that covers the nature of human existence. For example the psychological, religious, scientific and natural therapists, as well as the average person on the street, have different ways of explaining various mind phenomena. This is no more so than in our understanding of altered mind states.

My own journey of suffering from several mental disorders and then undergoing primal therapy created many different mind states and other unusual experiences. In my fifty something years of life I had only ever experienced my consciousness at the third level, which unbeknown to me, was interpreting my life from the desperate need to keep my primal pain at bay. Going through the second level of feelings and into the first level of consciousness and experiencing the sensations opened me up to different states of mind. I feel I am now in a good position to explain some of the differing mind states that can be produced by the human brain.

Exorcism

Definition – The ritualistic expulsion of evil spirits inhabiting the body, brain or place.

This definition would fit well with the description of a primal feeling. When I was conscious of sensing the pain of an unloved childhood, I was in no doubt that I was 'expelling evil spirits', although primal theory understands this process as feeling primal pain.

Stephen Diamond wrote an article titled *'Exorcism and the Endangered Future of Psychotherapy'* (www.psychology today.com/blog/evildeeds).

Diamond writes that the Roman Catholic Church is secretly educating a new crop of exorcists to meet rapidly rising demand for exorcisms in Italy, Australia, America and elsewhere around the globe.

Comment. The increase in demand for exorcism is most likely the result of the increase in mental disorders in the community in general. The demand will keep increasing until we understand the three levels of the human mind and how they function individually, and also how they interact together to form our conscious state. Only then will we be able to take effective steps to reduce the incidence of mental disorders.

My primal therapist was my 'exorcist'.

Diamond. *"Burgeoning numbers of suffering souls – some deeply disillusioned with or wary of what mainstream psychology and psychiatry have to offer, are desperately turning to exorcism to expel their debilitating devils and demons."*

Comment. 'Devils and demons' are primal pains trying to surface. The brains natural repressive mechanisms are being overwhelmed. Psychology and psychiatry do not have much to offer because they do not understand the three levels of consciousness and the power of the imprint. They are still operating within the third level of consciousness when the problem is on the first level, and they can never really understand this interaction between the three levels until they take that journey themselves.

Diamond. *"He talks of possession – what exactly is that? What is evil? Where does it come from? What is our relationship to it? Is it a proper subject of study for psychology and psychiatry? And how can we better deal with it."*

Comment. All these questions are answered when the journey from penthouse to basement, from third to second and down into the first level is taken. As I have stated, in my opinion they cannot be answered any other way other than by experience, because the first line speaks a powerful 'language' of sensations, unlike the third level language of words that we are so used to.

Possession is simply the brain holding onto primal pain, and the way to deal with it is to feel it in small increments.

And of course possession is a proper subject for psychology and psychiatry – primal pain (or possession) in my experience is the cause of almost all psychological and psychiatric disorders. Millions of people around the world are waiting, waiting, - for someone to understand their pain and take it away.

Diamond asks, *"Are demonic possession and mental illness the same thing? The subjective experience of possession – feeling influenced by some foreign, alien force beyond the ego's control – is to some extent, an experiential aspect of most mental disorders."*

Comment. Here we see evidence of how two differing organisations, those of the church and of psychology describe and treat the same phenomena in different ways. "An alien force beyond the ego's control" is one way I could have described my initial experiences of my first line of consciousness during primal therapy. There is no ego force on the first level of consciousness. Ego is entirely a function manifested at the third level, mostly to keep primal pain at bay. I now understand and experience my mind on the three distinct levels of consciousness, so their effects on my mind states are no longer alien to me. In fact I use this knowledge to my advantage in creating a better life for myself.

Diamond. *"Presently such disturbing symptoms are hypothesized by psychiatry to be due primarily to some underlying neurological or biochemical aberration. Biochemistry, in the form of the tiny neurotransmitter, has become our postmodern 'demon du jour' for which all manner of evils are blamed."*

Comment. While psychiatry remains an intellectual pursuit governed by the principals and needs of academia, it will always view the mind in a purely biological way. Our first level of consciousness is our spiritual side, our soul, our God like state of mind where most decisions about love, procreation and survival as a species are made. This system works extremely well provided the brain gets the right information handed down from the generations that have gone before. The intellectual way we have structured our lives in the present, as compared to 50,000 years ago, makes it difficult to transfer this information from one generation to the next. As I have stated before, this vital information cannot be transferred intellectually- it can only be achieved though sensations and feelings.

A person undergoing primal therapy also learns that neurotransmitters are just the messengers - the modifiers or enhancers of what we feel. They are not the original problem.

Diamond. *"If psychotherapy as a healing of the soul (not just the mind) is to survive and thrive in the future, our recent overemphasis on cognition, behaviour, genetics, neurology and biochemistry must be counterbalanced by the inclusion of the spiritual and depth psychological dimension of human existence."*

Comment. Our first level of consciousness gives us access to the spirituality and depth of meaning that Steve Diamond talks about. However I find it difficult to see a way forward unless all psychology and psychiatry students of the future are required to undergo primal therapy and have good access to all three levels of consciousness before they can go into clinical practise. Primal theory and therapy has the ability to bring all the differing viewpoints under one new paradigm, and I believe we will need to achieve this outcome if we as a species are to overcome our fatal flaw.

Diamond. *"They (the possessed) need a psychologically meaningful method to confront their metaphysical devils and demons, their repressed anger and rage, and the reality of evil. They need a secular psychotherapy willing to ask the right questions."*

Comment. In my experience we already have that in Janovian Primal Theory and Therapy. What we do not have is an accepted science of the first and second levels of consciousness that can prove it. However there is a large body of research that proves, or at least supports primal theory. The problem lies in the fact that academics and researchers, who have very strong third levels, cannot interpret their research in terms of first and second levels where, I believe, the devils and demons, repressed anger and rage and the source of all evil are generated.

Near death experiences (NDE's)

Eben Alexander is a neurosurgeon who suffered an attack of bacterial meningitis. He was unconscious for seven days, and during that time he says he experienced some fabulous things that led him to believe there is life after death. He then wrote a book called 'Proof of Heaven' which I have read. I am going to quote some of what he wrote, and then describe his experiences in terms of primal theory and therapy.

Alexander. *"I was struck by a rare illness and thrown into a coma for seven days. During that time my entire neo-cortex, the outer surface of the brain, the part that makes us human, was shut down – inoperative – in essence absent. When your brain is absent, you are absent too. During my coma my brain wasn't working improperly, it wasn't working at all."*

Comment. There are several misconceptions here. Firstly, implying that consciousness is what makes us human is true to a point, but what makes a human life worth living is generated in the subconscious. My experience is that love is the greatest feeling of all, and I believe this feeling starts as a sensation in the brainstem, which brings me to the second misconception. In the above quote, and in many others throughout the book, he tries to tell the reader he was totally absent, thereby inferring that his experiences were totally separate from his brain and body, hence his belief that there is life after death in a place called Heaven. But it appears his lower brains - his limbic system and brainstem - were still operating. His original coma was induced because of his uncontrollable epileptic type fits, so it was not a natural coma. He was put on a respirator for the duration of his induced coma in an effort to conserve his energy – this is also an important point because he still had a breathing reflex which means some parts of his brain must have been functioning. Also, as far as I can ascertain from his book, his heart was beating normally by itself, which also means his lower brain was still present and working.

I worked as a volunteer ambulance officer for twenty five years, and knowledge of a person's state of consciousness and level of brain functioning was drilled into us ad nauseam because if its importance. At no stage of Alexander's meningitis could he ever be classed as being dead. This is very important point because what Alexander experienced when in his medically induced coma was not life after death, but what happens when the third level of consciousness goes offline, and he gets to experience his first and second levels of consciousness in their pure form.

Alexander. *"I was encountering the reality of a world of consciousness that existed completely free of the limitations of my physical brain."*

Comment. What he could have said was when his prefrontal cortex shut down (which is responsible for his limited physical reality), he was able to directly experience the vastly different space and time that is generated by the lower brain.

Alexander. *"Those implications are tremendous beyond description – my experience showed me that the death of my body and brain are not the end of consciousness – that human experience continues beyond the grave."*

Comment. I am not sure how Alexander arrived at this conclusion. From what he reported in the book his body and brain were clearly not dead. He seems to be confusing unconsciousness with death; so here is an example of a very intelligent person's belief system not corresponding with scientific knowledge (see previous chapter). It is a scientific fact that the unconscious brain can be aware of and respond to its surroundings.

My mother had a fridge magnet in her house that said "I have made up my mind – don't confuse me with the facts." It seems to me that Alexander has made up his mind about life after death, and is not worrying about the facts.

E.A. *"The place I went to was real – real in a way that makes the life we are living here and now completely dreamlike by comparison."*

Comment. Of course the first level of consciousness is real, and when it is experienced it is certainly a huge contrast to the usual here and now.

E.A. *"At the same time my conclusions are based on a medical analysis of my experience, and on my familiarity with the most advanced concepts in brain science and consciousness studies."*

Comment. This statement sums up another reason I am writing this book. The most up to date science and analysis that Eben Alexander talks about does not include any understanding of the nature and power of brainstem functioning. Arthur Janov is famous for saying that if we catch the wrong train, then every station is wrong. The neuroscience and psychology industry needs to get off the train of intellect only, and jump on the train of feelings and sensations. For the sake of humanity let's all get on the right train.

Alexander. *" The (love) message had three parts*

(1) You are loved and cherished, dearly forever.

(2) You have nothing to fear.

(3) There is nothing that you can do wrong."

Comment. All these things describe the nature of love, and should exist in all close relationships, especially between intimate partners, and between parents and their children. These things also happen naturally from the power of the first level of consciousness. To say that another way, we don't have to *think* about correct action because the sensations of love will *drive* correct action.

Alexander. *"The primary hurdle that most Near Death Experiences (NDE) subjects must jump is not how to re-acclimatise to the limitations of the earthly world – though this can certainly be a challenge, but how to convey what the love they experienced out there actually felt like."*

Comment. I have experienced these things as well. I have spoken to doctors, psychologists and the general public about my experiences with primal therapy and all I get is a kind of blank stare. The more educated a person is the more they try to mould what I say into their own belief systems. Psychology calls this a person's personal schema, but it is my experience that during primal therapy I had to gradually dismantle my own schema's, and build completely new ones. I could salvage some old material to incorporate into my new understanding, but not much.

NDE subjects and primal patients get to experience the loving power of their brainstems, and then it is difficult to come back and live in a very neurotic, if not insane, world. It is difficult for myself and Eben Alexander to describe this experience in words, because words are the language of the third level of consciousness, whereas sensations and feelings of love have to be experienced to be understood. The loving world, or state of mind, that Alexander described is the one we all have the possibility of living in while on this earth.

Alexander. "*We can only see what our brain's filter allows through. The brain, in particular its left side linguistic/logical part, that which generates our sense of rationality and the feeling of being sharply defined ego or self – is a barrier to our higher knowledge and experience.*"

Comment. With this insight, Eben Alexander has eloquently described the action of the fatal flaw. Primal theory would describe the same action as the prefrontal cortex not allowing painful memories to come to consciousness and in the process blocks access to our 'higher knowledge and experience' that lies at our first level. Alexander's statement that our experience is governed by our brains filter is an extremely important one, and one that every person should understand when forming their own belief systems.

Alexander. "*Even on earth there is much more good than evil, but earth is a place where evil is allowed to gain influence in a way that would be entirely impossible at higher levels of existence.*"

Comment. Evil exists at the lower realm of human functioning, and once again using the GAL score as a reference, evil deeds increase as the GAL score decreases. There would be very little evil in this world if everybody had a GAL score of 80 or better. If the human race wants this outcome I believe it is possible in the here and now – we do not have to wait until after death.

Alexander. "*I was a citizen of a universe staggering in its vastness and complexity, and ruled entirely by love.*"

Comment. Once again this is a description of pure love as it is experienced in the first level of consciousness. Alexander had an NDE and I did primal therapy, and from his description we ended up in the same realm, or state of mind.

Alexander. "*What I had experienced was more real than the house I sat in, more real than logs burning in the fireplace. Yet there was no room for that reality in the medically trained scientific worldview that I'd spent years acquiring. How was I going to create room for both realities to co-exist*".

Comment. As I stated earlier, the scientific world view is on the wrong train. It is blindingly obvious to me, a layperson who has undergone the primal process that the concept of the triune brain, with the lower brains having the most influence in the way our lives are lived, will have to be the way of the future. Within this triune brain system there is room for only one reality, and that is the one that is driven by pure love. All advanced primal patients end up with a very different world view than the one they had previous to therapy.

Alexander. *"There was quite simply no way that my experiences, with the intensely sophisticated visual and aural levels and the high degree of perceived meaning, were the product of the reptilian portion of my brain."*

Comment. This is part of Alexanders' scientific world view and belief system/schema. My belief is that he is wrong! When a person undergoing primal therapy enters his brainstem/basement/first level of consciousness, he experiences the "intensely sophisticated visual and aural levels and the high degree of perceived meaning" coming from this space. The 'perceived meaning' part of Alexander's description is very important, because the brainstem sensations have that effect. We are used to experiencing meaning in terms of prefrontal cortex rationality and thoughts, but the sensations leave us with a 'sense' of what is true and real, which is difficult to put into words.

There seems to be a worldview that the brainstem is our animal side and therefore we should try and evolve past that side of human nature. Alexander's comment above is one such example, but I have also found this view to be common among scientists and lay people alike. It seems that somehow we should put all our effort into advancing our thinking brain and all human problems will be solved. But nothing is further from the truth. We already have everything that we need as humans in our present brains, and the brainstem is key to the existence that we as humans are looking for. It provides our spiritual side, it is our soul, it provides us with God-like powers – all we need is to have good access to its forces.

Alexander. *"Everything - the uncanny clarity of my vision, the cleanness of my thought as pure conceptual flow – suggested higher, not lower brain function. But my higher brain function had not been around to do the work."*

Comment. But his lower brains were still functioning, and the cleanness and realness is what the lower brain deals in – sensations and feelings are real and clear because they are not cluttered with the filtered worldview and belief systems that the human prefrontal cortex struggles with.

When having a near death experience, a person goes directly from their prefrontal cortex worldview into their brainstem reality. They jump the gap between thinking and sensation/feeling, and so do not understand where they are, hence Eben Alexander believing he was in Heaven. People undergoing primal therapy take the slow journey from their prefrontal cortex reality, down through their feelings and eventually, after many months, enter the sensations. Traumatic imprinting causes much pain, and when entering this space, or level of consciousness, it seems like a good representation of hell (personal experience). But as the primal pain is released, entering this space becomes more like heaven (also personal experience).

Tienke Klein, Holocaust survivor and her NDE experience.

A blaze of light appeared and she felt an energy pervading everything, including herself. *"I was completely that energy"* she said, *"It was love, it was wisdom, it was dynamism."* She received all the answers to her questions at once. *"I was happy, so incredibly happy."*

When she regained consciousness, a resonance of the experience remained. She felt lonely when she realized the things people around her were talking about had no substance in comparison to the profound truth she had just experienced.

Comment - To me this is just another description of experiencing the best of the first level of consciousness, and then coming back and having trouble trying to live at the level most humans are operating at in the present time.

Interesting new research

Scientists from Northwestern University found that amino acids (glutamate and GABA) also help encode memories of a fear-inducing event, and hides these memories away from the conscience. *"The brain functions in a different state, much like a radio operates at AM and FM frequency bands"*, said principal investigator Dr Jelena Radulovic, the Dunbar Professor in Bipolar Disease at Northwestern University Feinberg School of Medicine. *"It's as if the brain is normally tuned to FM stations to access memories, but needs to be tuned to AM stations to access subconscious memories."*

This is a good description of how primal therapy works. We start life at the AM frequency (sensations) and then develop our FM stations (cognition). When we suffer trauma early in life we leave our

AM (sensations) behind and live in the relative comfort of the FM frequency. If we want to deal with childhood trauma later in our lives we have to go back and tune into the AM band. That is what primal therapy does. When I switched frequency during my own therapy (connected to the past) it felt like every cell in my body fired. The exciting thing about this new research is that it helps to prove that humans do operate at different levels, realms or frequencies. It is also another example showing that research results can make more sense if interpreted with an understanding of primal theory and the three levels of consciousness.

A stroke experience

Jill Bolte Taylor is a neuroscientist who gave a TED talk (on the internet) entitled *"My Stroke of Insight"*. Taylor had a stroke in her left hemisphere, and the blood clot produced was about the size of a golf ball. These are some of the things she experienced before the operation to remove the blood clot.

The left hemisphere says we are separate from each other. The right hemisphere feels we are all the same and we are connected to each other. Jill was shocked to find herself not able to think. For example the stress from her job was gone and she felt very peaceful.

"I found nirvana and my consciousness expanded". (I would suggest she tuned into her AM band)

Comment. In this case Jill Taylor did not go unconscious as with an NDE, but she did lose a lot of her left brain function. This apparently left her brain open to experiencing the right hemisphere, or feeling side of her brain. As you can probably see, her concept of nirvana and expanded consciousness is similar to what Eben Alexander and Tienke Klein have experienced.

Near the end of her talk, Jill Taylor says we have the choice to step into our right hemisphere, but in my opinion, this shows Jill's ignorance about the true situation. We do not have that choice because of the defence system that keeps us from our primal pain. Using the house analogy, people do not dare leave the penthouse and enter the basement because it contains too much pain. Primal therapy gives a person the chance to enter their basement, but it is a long and painful journey. To say we have a choice just to step from one level of consciousness to another is a gross misrepresentation of what is actually happening. She did not just step, she suffered a stroke which closed down most of her third level cognitive brain, which allowed the feeling right-side brain to dominate. Jill got to experience the joy of her first level of consciousness, but I would not recommend having a stroke as the best means of doing so.

Recreational drugs

From author Fitz Hugh Ludlow's book "The Hasheesh Eater"(1857).

"Drugs are able to bring humans into the neighbourhood of divine experience and can thus carry us up from our personal fate and the everyday circumstances of our life into a higher form of reality. It is, however, necessary to understand precisely what is meant by the use of drugs. We do not mean purely physical craving, ... that of which we speak is something much higher, namely the knowledge of the possibility of the soul to enter into a higher being, and to catch a glance, a glimpse of higher insights and more magnificent visions of beauty, truth, and the divine than we are normally able to spy through the cracks in our prison walls."

This was written in 1857, so even back then people were taking recreational drugs in an effort to alter their states of mind to a more divine level. The present day illegal drugs epidemic would suggest we have not progressed very far down the path of understanding the underlying causes and effects of drug addiction. Drugs like heroin and methamphetamine are used to induce mind states that have been described in similar ways to how people describe NDE's.

Then there are the drugs that psychiatrists and doctors prescribe by the tens of millions. These drugs may be classed as legal medicines, but their function is still the same – to alter a person's state of mind. For example people who suffer from depression and anxiety do not wish to put up with these mind states, so they take drugs to try and alter the situation they find themselves in.

The similarity of NDE's and other altered mind states

Medical Doctor Jeffrey Long wrote a book called 'Evidence of the Afterlife; The Science of Near Death Experience.' In the book, Long contends his studies of over thirteen hundred people show that accounts of near death experience play out remarkably similarly among the people who had them. The accounts cross age and cultural boundaries to such a degree that they can't be chalked up simply to everyone having seen the same Hollywood movie. Some of the similarities are as follows,

• Crystal clear recollection

• Heightened senses

- Re-union with deceased family members
- Long lasting effects after the person is brought back to life.
- A feeling of ecstasy, nirvana, and above all, Love, or the presence of a loving human being
- An expanded consciousness

Comment. The similarity of experiences could be put down to evolution, in that our brainstems evolved over a period of millions of years, and so our brainstems all work in exactly the same way. This situation may not be clear to people who constantly live in the third level of consciousness, because at this level we all vary greatly in belief systems and schemas that develop from our personal experiences. Dr Long touches on an important understanding of the brainstem when he says NDE's cross age and cultural barriers. The brainstem does not recognise people as being different, it only acts at a species level; that is its actions are powerful in procreation and the ability to survive. Therefore, at the first level of consciousness there is no racism, no differing religious views, no hate, no mental disorders and no class differences. There is only the experience of pure love which drives our procreation and our ability to care for ourselves and others, so that we survive as a species.

Pure love gives a person all the answers they need, highlighted senses that give a crystal clear perception and a very holistic world view; all these elements are described in various ways by those who have had an NDE, others who have experienced various altered mind states, and those who are advanced patients of primal therapy.

An NDE is something that happens before death. When a person passes from life to death the death experience may be something else entirely. My own personal belief is that we go back to what we were – ashes to ashes, dust to dust. From my own understanding nobody has ever came back from death to tell the rest of us what death is like. I want to make this point very strongly because, in my experience, an NDE produces a mind state that is possible in this life. We do not have to wait until death to have these wonderful mind states that are described in so much of the NDE literature. In my opinion all the experiences described by Long are functions of the brainstem. This fact has not been proven by science yet because they do not seem to understand the principals involved. Remember that Eben Alexander, a Harvard Professor, said he can't relate his scientific learning and world view to the experience of his NDE, but it is no mystery to a person who has experienced the actions of the different parts of the triune brain.

Just to remind readers, the fatal flaw is the disconnection between the pre-frontal cortex and the brainstem. NDE's have given many people a glimpse of what is possible in this life. As a species we need to understand that our higher selves – that which many people seek – actually resides with-in our lower brains in the here and now.

Long reports in his book that millions of people worldwide have had NDE's, and millions more are afraid to say anything, because the force of the experience scared them, or that they will be ridiculed if they talk openly about their experiences. As a society it is very unfortunate that we do not understand the phenomenon for what it is.

Not all experiences of altered mind states are of the loving kind. A small percentage of experiences include a description of the horror and awfulness that is similar to what a primal patient goes through when dealing with primal pain. I can offer no explanation as to why most people experience a loving type of altered mind state while unconscious, while others suffer the horror that exists in a traumatised brainstem, but I am sure there is one. Maybe the mind is like a roulette wheel, with the chances heavily stacked towards love, and if you spin 'fear and horror' it is just not your night!

The God Force

Now I will bring a discussion of God into the equation. From my research on the internet this is how some people view God.

"God is a reality that words alone cannot adequately describe. Most of the time we have descriptive words such as Love, Life, Light, All Source, Force, One, Mind, Conscious, Vibration, Spirit, Being, etc. But according to many experiences even these descriptions are woefully inadequate. The memories of these other experiences beat all others hands down, for their vivid sense of reality. The difference was so vast."

Someone else wrote – *"Life is Love is God" If you add anymore to this definition then you are not making it any better.*

Comment. However I would add feeling to the above and change the order to Love is a Feeling, is God, is Life. If we don't have love, then we don't have anything, or in so many cases not a life worth living anyway. Love is not esoteric or something to think about, it is a sensation/feeling, and the difference is expressed by one of the above writers when he finishes with *"The difference is so vast"*.

That difference is the outcome of the fatal flaw. Mankind has removed himself so far from his natural feeling state and into his intellect that it is difficult to return, or even realise that love exists in such a powerful state. Those who have NDE's and other altered states of mind are returning to that pure feeling state, but no one seems to recognise these states for what they are.

I think that most of the world's population would agree that there are some forces within our minds that we do not understand, and in the absence of any other plausible explanation, mankind has invented, with his intellect, the notion of an omniscient (all knowing), omnipresent (everywhere at all times) and omnipotent (all powerful) being and called it God.

So now I can give two explanations for God, one on the third level of consciousness which is a belief system based on faith, and the other is the God like energy of pure love and I will compare them.

The God of the prefrontal cortex or third level has given rise to what is generally known as religion. This religion is faith based, in that there is no scientific evidence of a God. It comes under my description of a false belief system. There are hundreds of different religions in the world, and many of them say that only *their* followers will go to an afterlife. They can't all be right with that particular belief!

Religion in its various forms has been around for centuries and yet it has not proven itself to be inherently moral, altruistic, or acted as a unifying force for all living creatures on this earth. Religion has some good moral underpinnings but most of them fall by the wayside in practice. For example the Catholic Church is rife with paedophilia, the Catholics and Protestants killing each other in Ireland and the Muslims and Jews constantly at war. The Muslims legalise killing by saying it is their God given right to kill the infidels and they also kill to protect family honour. The God of faith (of the prefrontal cortex) is full of ideas and beliefs, and not all of these are proving to be helpful in our evolution or giving us a peaceful life in the present. As a species we need to understand that ideas and beliefs, if generated from a traumatically imprinted brainstem, will not give humans a good moral base.

The God of the brainstem, or first level of consciousness, is very much like the descriptions of people who have experienced altered states of mind. It is not faith based or connected with a belief system.

From my own experience during primal therapy, there were times when I became aware that there was a part of my brain doing its own thing, and it was best for my therapy to let it be my guide. In other words I felt I had another 'unconscious' intelligence that was different and stronger than my prefrontal cortex capabilities. This 'God force' and/or 'primal intelligence' is somehow, I believe, embedded in our DNA, and shows itself through sensations that turn to feelings of love, and these feelings provide for our moral code. This moral code has been built up over millions of years, and rather than arising from part of our brain that some scientists and sociologists now believe is an animal encumbrance from our past, it still provides a very strong basis for our continuing evolution. If we do not reconnect with this part of our brain then human evolution may not continue – the fatal flaw.

When viewing the brain as three separate areas we can see that religion is a product of the prefrontal cortex. Therefore it suffers from many false beliefs and the fanaticism of a mind that needs to keep itself separated from reality, especially the reality of a traumatised brainstem – the destructive, divisive, anti-evolutionary force.

Our true moral laws, spirituality, altruistic nature, love, God force, - whatever you want to call it - reside at the first level of consciousness – the unifying pro-evolutionary force.

In every individual a spiritual element is manifested

Leo Tolstoy

Christopher Hitchens wrote a book called "God is Not Great". Within its pages he details a lot of the un-Godly deeds that have been perpetrated on humanity in the name of religion. The western world is currently running a war against what it labels as terrorism, but it is my understanding the combined religions of the world are causing a lot more human suffering and death than the so-called terrorists. Religion has always been difficult to criticise because it claims the moral high ground and therefore its views should be sacrosanct.

Hitchens writes *"Those who believe that the existence of conscience is a proof of a godly design are advancing an argument that simply cannot be disproved because there is no evidence for or against it"*.

And in the last chapter (19) titled 'In Conclusion; The Need for a New Enlightenment.' *Religion has run out of justifications. Thanks to the telescope and the microscope, it no longer offers an explanation of anything important. Where once it used to be able, by its total command of a worldview to prevent the emergence of rivals, it can now only impede and retard – or try to turn back the measureable advances we have made.'*

In my experience primal theory and primal therapy, which are based on the three powerful and separate levels of brain functioning, offers a doorway into the new enlightenment that Hitchens talks about.

With the understanding that a God like code may be embedded in our DNA, we don't have to have faith that a higher force rules our lives - we actually have a way of experiencing that force and letting it direct our lives. That force really is omniscient, omnipresent and omnipotent. One day scientists will find a way of proving the existence of the forces generated from the first level of consciousness, and then God and science will come together. I see it as the only way that humanity will be able to live peacefully and healthfully.

And now abide faith, hope and love, these three; but the greatest of these is love.

1. Corinthians 13:13 NKJV

TRUTH AND TRUST

Each and every species of life on this planet has developed a survival strategy that aims to ensure the continuation for that particular species. For example the cactus plant has developed sharp spines so grazing animals leave them alone, and they also have the ability to store moisture in a harsh desert environment. School fish and insects that are heavily consumed by predators can survive as a species because of their prodigious numbers and ability to breed rapidly when circumstances are right. Crocodiles survive as individuals because of their size, protective skin and powerful jaws, while giraffes use their height to advantage in being able to graze at a higher level than other animals.

As humans we survived as a species because we formed social groups. Within these groups people had a specific role to play, depending on their age and gender. Babies and infants renewed the species, older children learnt the ways of the group and developed their survival skills, firstly through play and then more serious activities, mothers nurtured the children and gathered food, and fathers provided food and protection. Elders provided the wisdom of how to survive in the local environment, as well as still contributing as active members of the group. Group survival was more important than individual needs. As part of that survival strategy we came to depend on each other to tell the *truth* and to have *trust* in each other. As an example, a mother needed to have trust that her partner and other members of the group would provide a safe environment for the nurturing of children. The younger members trusted that the elders knew where and when to seek seasonal food sources and what the dangers were in the local environment.

The truth of any situation was relayed to other members of the group so that everyone knew what was happening. For example if someone found a food source such as a berry patch, then everyone else was informed; the finder did not keep the berries to themselves. If somebody spotted danger then they had a way of conveying that to others in the group. We can observe these behaviours in many of the mammal groups in the wild today.

The human species has evolved in an environment of truth and trust in each other that has been part of a survival strategy in what can sometimes be a hostile environment. Even in the present day we seem to have an innate understanding that those around us will tell the truth, and that we can trust them to do the right thing by us. Obviously this is not a real strength within our present culture, and letting this particular survival mechanism slip in importance may reduce our chances of long term survival.

Love is a pure sensation that generates a certain state of mind; one that has the quality of being all powerful and unshakeable. Sometimes it is said that it is best not to tell the truth, because some people cannot handle the truth. But pure love has the quality of handling any truth, because love is the most powerful truth of all and cannot be usurped by any lesser truths, and certainly not lies.

While my argument for the evolutionary importance of truth and trust in our daily lives may not be on solid scientific grounds, I believe that they are somehow encoded in our DNA, so we must have lived through a large part of our evolution in an environment of truth and trust. One writer on the web put it like this '*A golden age where rights and trusts were cultivated without the constraints of law; an age of innocence*'. (The reference to law is quite pertinent because our society has created a huge and lucrative industry for itself to deal with breaches of truth and trust).

To support my theory about how truth and trust are encoded in our DNA and form part of our survival mechanism, I will discuss some current research on two specific hormones, both of which are involved in sex (procreation) and social bonding. Both sex and social bonding are involved in our successful evolution.

Neuroscientist Bernd Weber studied the effects of testosterone on trustworthiness of men. This male hormone boosts libido and builds muscle, and is often associated with aggression and antisocial behaviour. But testosterone fuelled hunks may also be less likely to lie and cheat than some of their brothers, the research suggests. In a controlled gaming test, the men who had been given testosterone patches were less likely to cheat than those given a placebo. The authors concluded that the results clearly contradict the one-dimensional approach that testosterone results in anti-social behaviour. They showed that testosterone also acted in the realm of truth and trust.

Oxytocin is more commonly known as the hormone of love, but it is also being researched for its effects on the ability of a person to trust. Larry Young, a researcher at Emory University in Atlanta has this to say, *"The effects we're seeing from oxytocin today are really just the tip of the iceberg. Instead of getting them to sniff the obvious bottle of oxytocin, we could put a pill in their coffee and cause their brains to be flooded with oxytocin. You're not getting a truth serum, but you're getting them to trust you."*

From a personal level, when I looked at the research on oxytocin, I was dismayed that much of the focus was on using oxytocin as an interrogation drug – it does not seem right to me to use the love hormone in this way.

Jonathon Moreno, a bioethicist with the University of Pennsylvania – *"It seems on the face of it more humane (than torture) but on the other hand, in its own way it's another way of undermining human dignity. If you're using a chemical, you're losing control over who you are. It somehow gets to a deeper level of what it means to be a person"* he says.

The above observation is an accurate description of what oxytocin does naturally in the human body. When oxytocin flows in the body it means we have access to our deeper, more meaningful selves, and the effect is so strong that it seems like we are "losing control over who we are." But this action is a good one – give me a rush of natural oxytocin any day – it is how I want to experience this world.

The problem with humanity is that many people are repressing primal pain, and therefore do not have access to the flow of oxytocin and their deeper selves. Having access to our deeper feelings is so important in good human relationships. If scientists could find a way to get everybody's oxytocin to flow naturally, then maybe we wouldn't need so much interrogation of individuals (by making this statement I am implying that loving people, who have a good flow of oxytocin, would not commit the crimes in the first place, and so interrogation would not be needed).

So it seems to me truth and trust are encoded in the human DNA and their effects on our behaviour are facilitated by the release of testosterone and oxytocins.

In my work as a primal therapist I quite often have patients who try to suppress parts of their previous behaviour or thoughts because they are embarrassed at what they have done. These embarrassing thoughts and behaviours are part of a person's defence system, and most people undergoing primal therapy have to face, at some stage, the reality of their previous neurotic actions. Eventually the force of the need to tell the truth overcomes any embarrassment, and the truth is then told. Once the truth is out the patient usually feels great relief and then therapy can proceed to other matters.

In the usual scheme of things, the truth, once expressed, loses its importance. This reminds me of several quotes I have read in other places. *'Truth will out. One way or another, in spite of all efforts to conceal it, the truth will come to be known.'* and also *'And ye shall know the truth, and the truth shall set you free.'*

One problem with the brainstem and its sensing apparatus is that it hangs on to old truths as if they are still real in the present. For example my father threatened my life on many occasions, so I grew up with the belief he was going to kill me. This meant I was always anxious and wary around men, especially those who looked like my father. By the time I started primal therapy my father had been dead for thirty years, but the memory of the terror was still imprinted in my brain, and was still affecting my life in so many negative ways. Once the terror of those memories was relived my mind could finally relax.

During primal therapy, facing the truth of a situation is the difficult and painful part. In my case the truth was my mother looked after my physical body but not my spiritual side, and my father either ignored me or belted me for mostly minor indiscretions. I grew up being scared to do anything for fear of doing it wrong and being punished. The benefits of facing the horrible truth of my past sets me free in ways I could never have dreamed of.

When belief systems become cultural truths

Truth and trust are important ideals in a human life but quite often the belief systems we adopt to avoid feeling our primal pains are not compatible with these ideals. If we fully understand and experience the power of brainstem sensations we realise that these sensations have the ability to create a very deep sense of love that can also be described as our spiritual side. If we are connected to this deep feeling within, it gives us a sense of being fulfilled, happiness in our own skin, and of not wanting to be or attain something else. But when we carry primal pain the brain keeps us from accessing these painful memories by blocking the pathways to it, and these are the same pathways to our loving feelings and deeper selves. For some people life can still be a reasonably good experience, but increasing numbers of people are becoming aware that something is missing, that life has no meaning, and many others put up with various levels of mental disorders such as depression and anxiety. At the extreme level some people are suffering so badly that they decide to suicide.

Our society has developed many ways to try and fill the void that exists within a separated brain. One of the most popular and lucrative forms is for people to write self-help books about how to make sense of a difficult and meaningless life, and then give instructions on how to attempt to fill that void within. Some of the most popular examples are *'The Five Love Languages'* by Gary Chapman, *'The Four Agreements'* by Don Miguel Ruiz, *'Conversations with God'* by Neal Donald Walsch, and *'Proof of Heaven'* by Eben Alexander.

Gary Chapman suggests there are five love languages, but in my experience love has only one language, and that it speaks to us through pure sensation. We then perform various actions out of a sensation/ feeling of love, so things like giving of gifts, quality time, words of affirmation, touch and acts of service (the five languages) are things we do automatically *because* we are in love.

If you decide your predominant love language is quality time for example, it may be a neurotic need stemming from the fact your parents didn't spend quality time with you. You then need your partner close at all times, but however much time they give it still does not fill the void within. Acts of love that are generated from an intellectual understanding of love are *forced* behaviours that take a lot of maintaining and focus and are not always successful because they may become robotic – that is - without feeling. As a contrast acts of love that come from a sensation are automatic and without effort, and are delivered with a feeling that the receiver can perceive as love.

Don Ruiz suggests we can live by four agreements as a way of directing our lives.

- Be impeccable with your word

- Don't take anything personally

- Don't make assumptions

- Always do your best

The four agreements are worthy guides to live by, but are really just ways of experiencing love in its pure form. That is, if we have access to our loving selves we do all those things automatically. We don't have to make agreements with anybody or anything.

One of the agreements is not to make assumptions, but we all make assumptions in one way or another. The problem is not in making the assumption, but in regarding assumptions as truth, and then act on the assumption as if it is the truth. A small example is the fact I like fried eggs on toast, and so someone cooks me scrambled eggs on toast, which I don't like, and when I complain they say "I assumed you would also like scrambled eggs on toast". This may seem like a petty example, but I have had these annoying experiences in my life, and also see it happen quite often in other situations. At the other end of the scale people can get killed by others making wrong assumptions about a situation. Saddam Hussein and the 'weapons of mass destruction' he was supposed to be hiding in Iraq are a well known example.

Don Ruiz also suggests to always do your best, but how is my 'best' defined these days. Is it a well paid job with long hours or is it taking my son fishing. Being the best worker may mean 60 hours a week on the job, while being the best parent may mean less work hours and more time with family. On occasion I just like to flop on the lounge and watch television; is that my best effort?

My definition of being my best is to keep raising my GAL score. From this position everything else in my life falls into place. But the only way to keep raising my GAL score is to feel my primal pain, not by reading psychology or self help books. If a person happens to be lucky enough to have a high GAL score then the four agreements are part of how that person will conduct their life. They don't need to read books on how to live their lives because it will happen naturally in a fulfilling way.

When Eben Alexander describes his near death experience in terms of an afterlife, what he is describing is the nature of brainstem sensations (see earlier chapter). When Walsch talks about his conversations with God, he is describing how all humans should take notice of their inner voice, which is generated from the brainstem and comes to us through the feelings of pure love. Until we understand that the brainstem can generate such psychological power, our understanding of the causes and cures of mental health will remain in the dark ages.

Regarding the issues of truth and trust, the authors of the above books, in my opinion, are doing their best in explaining the human condition with the knowledge they have. They are not deliberately withholding facts, they may just not be aware of them. Many people need to seek help in understanding the human condition, and these types of books are widely read for that purpose. Self help books can give people a better understanding of how life works, and also give them a toolbox of options for living a better life ('toolbox of options' has become a common psychological term for using a shotgun approach to cures in mental health - if you fire enough cures their way something is bound to work a little bit). However they all remain in the realm of trying to fix symptoms that occur in the prefrontal cortex, while not being aware of the need to reduce primal pain as the only way to a more meaningful and loving life. And if anyone wants to argue that self help books have been of great benefit to themselves or others then that is fine, but be aware you are probably selling yourself well short of what is possible in this life. I believe there is a greater truth than the one these authors' write about.

The danger in self help books is that people start adopting things like 'The Five Love Languages' and 'The Four Agreements' as some sort of ultimate truth that then become embedded as cultural truths. Then babies, whose only need is pure love, maybe born into that society and only receive dogma. I know this first hand because many of the people I have been through therapy with and also the patients I treat have been severely traumatised by religious dogma and other beliefs that are not based on the experience of pure love.

Even so people are always doing their best. We can land a man on the moon and send gigabytes of information around the world in fractions of a second, but we do not understand what real love is, let alone knowing how to practise it in our daily lives.

Is it any wonder that the world has so many dysfunctional brains? ·

Not telling the truth by omission of known facts

The effectiveness of advertising relies largely on not telling the whole truth. Most advertising highlights the most positive aspect of a product without mentioning any negatives. For example fast food outlets dominate the food advertising landscape, highlighting flavour, price, convenience and the 'in' thing to do, without mentioning the lack of healthy food choices and the overuse of packaging.

Vitamin and mineral supplements and their advertising is a cause of much angst for me, as they are a prime example of not telling the whole truth by omission of known facts.

While studying naturopathy in 2001/2002 our class went to a supplement factory. The thing I remember most were the dozens of 20 litre plastic buckets that were full of a white powder. At the time I had visions of healing my own life and then making a career out of helping others. There is a truism that broken people are the ones who become most passionate about fixing others! I came away from that supplement factory very disillusioned, knowing at an intuitive level that buckets of white powder were not going to cure my problems or anyone else's.

One of the ways to sell supplements is to claim that our soils are either poor or are being stripped of their natural nutrients by modern farming methods. This claim always bothered me because I came from a farming community that used fertiliser with added trace elements. Accurate testing became available to check that the soil had a balance of nutrients to support healthy plant growth. I am aware of the debate between chemical and organic fertilisers, but I could be forgiven for being confused by the many people who don't agree with using chemical fertilisers, but are taking handfuls of chemicals daily in the form of supplements.

The supplement manufacturers point to many trials that show the benefits of taking supplements. Even before I studied statistics as part of my psychology course, there were two aspects of the research that bothered me. The first issue was that a lot of the research was done on people who were already sick, and the possibility they were sick because of a poor diet was high. In this case taking supplements may have corrected some deficiencies in their diet, thereby giving a reasonable statistical result.

Some good results are also seen within the general population, but it is well known that the western diet is full of calories and very low in nutrition. For example an advertising campaign to promote the 5 veg and two fruits plus nuts and seeds diet was a waste of money – a follow up survey found that 95% of Australians still do not eat the five plus two diet. Therefore people who are low on nutrients like calcium, iron, folate, zinc, and vitamins which are all available in a healthy balanced diet, may show improvement in functioning when they take supplements.

The second aspect of supplement research that bothers me is that there should be a control group of unhealthy people who are given a healthy diet to see how they change in comparison to the supplement only group. Have you ever seen a headline that states 'supplements more beneficial than a healthy diet in treating cancer (or any other disease)'? I certainly haven't! In any case I feel that getting a group of people to change from a poor diet to a healthy diet in a matter of weeks for research purposes would be almost impossible. Many of our junk food choices are really psychological addictions, and when addictions are stopped it allows the primal pain to come to consciousness, so we either have to feel the pain or go back to eating junk food. In my own case it took a combination of extensive learning about food and what it contained, as well as undergoing primal therapy to reduce my primal pain before my diet could improve to where it is today. And this process did not take weeks but years, because the society I was born into imprinted a lot of tampered information into my brain that was ultimately not in my best interest. I have learnt the hard way that our culture does not always deal in the truth, and therefore cannot always be trusted.

The advertising industry has been so effective in its campaign that it is hard to walk into a house that does not contain a quantity of supplement containers. Supplements are an expensive way of eating food, and I will spend my money on buying almonds, pumpkin seeds and blueberries, plus my five veg and two fruits.

The supplement industry is just one example of people manipulating the truth for profit, without caring how it affects people. We should be living in a society where people will tell the truth no matter what, and be able to trust that the actions of others are in the best interests of the whole group.

Propaganda

Propaganda is telling people only what you want them to know, or to embellish the facts of a certain stance etc. It is used quite widely in government and political circles at all levels, and Adolph Hitler of World War 11 fame became well known for his large and aggressive propaganda department.

Propaganda can sometimes be amusing in its obvious ridiculousness, such as in what passes for information coming out of North Korea. An example – their esteemed leader was reported to have made eleven holes in one on his first round of golf!

On a more personal level I lived on Kangaroo Island, which is situated off southern Australia. During their annual migration Southern Right whales could be seen from the shores of this island, so I developed a love and awe of these great beasts. The Japanese started to hunt (mostly Mincke) whales in the Southern Ocean, and so Australia complained to the International Whaling Commission. Japan asserted they were killing whales for research, which was allowed under the whaling agreement. But I took that bit of propaganda as an insult to my intelligence, because why would scientists need to kill hundreds of whales for research purposes? Where was their logic for needing to kill so many whales?

Also on another personal note I believe that moderate Muslims claiming that Islam is a peaceful religion is a piece of dangerous propaganda. 'Fatwahs' and 'killing the infidels' are written into their 'constitution', and both are practised daily by those who are deemed to be radicals.

Quran 2: 191-193 'And kill them wherever you find them, and turn them out from where they have turned you out...'

Quran (8:12) 'I will cast terror into the hearts of those who disbelieve. Therefore strike off their heads and strike off their fingertips...'

Quran (8:67) 'It is not for a Prophet that he should have prisoners of war until he had made a great slaughter in the land...'

There are many more such verses in the Quran that encourage followers of Islam to kill and maim disbelievers. I believe that unless the moderates act to remove the religiously motivated killing that is contained in Sharia law, we have on earth the possibility of propaganda aiding in the killing of more 'infidels' than Hitler's propaganda aided in killing Jews. The nature of pure love, which all humans have the ability to feel, including Nazi's and radical Muslims, does not contain the right to kill others.

Evil is restrained not with violence but with love.

It is natural for men to help and to love one another,

but not to torture and to kill one another.

Leo Tolstoy

The Chinese government is also known for its propaganda. In a communist regime freedom of the press is not allowed, and with freedom goes truth and trust. The Chinese can hide many things, such as abusing individual rights and letting corruption within the party go unchecked. Their propaganda department puts out press releases and makes films and documentaries that give a very one-sided view of life in a communist country.

Even the democratic capitalist countries of the so called western world, including Australia in which I live, resort to the use of propaganda when they feel the need.

I have tried to show in this chapter that truth and trust has been a necessary part of successful human evolution. The thing about telling the truth is that once the truth is confronted, we have to face the consequences, and generally humans are not good at that. In the examples given above, if the Muslims said "Yes, part of our religion is violent because we are allowed to kill the infidels, and to uphold family honour we have to kill our daughters if they fall in love with a Christian boy," then they are more likely to try and eradicate that part of their belief system and become a truly peaceful religion. If the Chinese opened up their press and told people the facts, then they would have to do something about the lack of personal freedoms.

In the United States, which likes to see itself as the doyen of freedom and civil liberties, they have huge social problems, largely because they confuse religious beliefs with love. They have the freedom of the individual enshrined in a Bill of Rights without understanding that at a personal level our first actions as a human must be for the survival of the species as a whole. This may seem like the individual has to subjugate themselves to the needs of the community, but evolution has given us a reward for that in the nature of the love we experience when we help our fellow man.

The problem is not really one of being Communist, a greedy Capitalist, Muslim or any other belief system. *The problem with all of humanity is primal pain that blocks access to love, and therefore it is the mind of man and the way it has evolved that is the underlying problem.*

The problem of not knowing a greater truth

My journey to good mental health through primal therapy, and experiencing the three levels of consciousness has delivered to me a greater truth than is currently known, I believe, by most of the mental health professionals and also the general population. For example there is a common saying among professionals when they talk about anxiety and depression. "Depression and anxiety are highly treatable". This statement may have some truth but it has a high degree of propaganda and positive spin as well. They couldn't cure my depression nearly twenty years ago, and nothing much in their treatment plans has changed since. I have met many people who suffer anxiety and depression whom the medical profession cannot help. It is easy to find websites of professionals that are in despair of their inability to treat these two common afflictions with anything that may resemble a cure. The following was written by Michael J Meaney, PhD, on the Psychology Today website.

"Depression is one of the most common and serious illnesses in the world, but sadly also the most mysterious. Experts still do not know what causes the illness, how to diagnose it physically, or treat it effectively. However we can garner important information by studying depression in families".

As the reader can probably understand the above statement only deals in the truth from a cognitive perspective.

From my personal experiences a statement more closely aligned to the underlying truth of the situation would be "We have treatment plans that can reduce the intensity and duration of your disorder, or activities that help you manage your disorder, but if you want a cure for your depression then the only option we have at the moment is to undergo a therapy that deals with primal pain. That pain was likely imprinted when your needs where not met during your childhood. Your parents may have done the best they could, but it is difficult to raise a healthy, feeling child when we live in a society that venerates wealth and power, and has little understanding of the power of love in human lives."

In the fuller statement above we are confronted with a deeper truth. We know that if we have a disorder we have a choice of palliation or cure. Twenty years ago I was only offered palliation, and nobody could tell me why I had the disorders I had. When we are aware of the causes we also have the options. For example if we know that deficits in parenting can cause mental illness, will we keep going down the same materialistic path, or will we restructure our entire society to suit the needs of parents to provide a loving environment for their children? Some of the Scandinavian countries have taken note of the research that shows poor or absent parenting causes many psychological problems, and are already restructuring their economic and social systems.

Special note - I am not saying that my truth regarding primal therapy and theory and the three levels of consciousness is the ultimate truth, but in my experience it is a huge advance on the understanding of human nature and mental illness that we have at the present time. Having said that I am not sure we will ever advance past expressing pure love, nor will we need to.

(N B. If you suffer from depression or anxiety please seek help. The act of talking to someone about your problems helps to get it off your chest, and the treatments available do have some success. In writing the above I am trying to put a perspective on the current situation and then compare that to what is possible with primal therapy. In a truly loving world depression and anxiety would not exist, but that world is probably a long way into the future. Meanwhile we have to manage things as best we can).

Raising children in truth and trust

"The first real choice a human baby must make is whether to trust or mistrust other humans. This basic trust versus mistrust stage is the first building block upon which all later love relationships are formed" (Dr Ken Magid and Carole McKelvey in *High Risk*).

Children need to develop in an environment of truth and trust. Our survival depends on our parents so we have to trust that they will care for us. My father was a very irrational man, and sometimes he belted me for what I thought were minor infractions, and he physically abused my mother. I grew up not trusting that my father would protect me, and that was how I came to view most men. If we grow up not trusting our parents it becomes difficult to trust anyone with our lives again. In severe cases such as is seen in Borderline Personality Disorder, relationships with others become almost impossible because the sufferer is paranoid about being mistreated. This very defensive and untrusting stance drives potential friends and partners away.

We also misunderstand the ability of children to accept the truth, and what effect withholding the truth has on the child. One example is when a family member dies and the parents try to protect the child by not talking about the situation openly, by not asking how the child feels, or not letting them go to the funeral. Feeling grief is part of being human and, I believe, if it is suppressed it will make the physical body sick in some way. These unresolved issues quite often come up during the process of primal therapy, and the patient is surprised when they fall into a long and painful crying session over someone who died perhaps thirty years ago. It is always a huge relief to let go, and for many it is the opportunity to finally say goodbye to a loved one.

Another common example is the trauma, secrecy and lies that surround many acrimonious divorces. Generally children will still love and need both parents, so using your children to try to win points against your partner confuses the child. Quite often they are also feeling that they are the cause of the divorce, and also suffer stress because they lose a parent from their lives. It is important to be open and honest with any children and realise that they have feelings of their own. As a therapist I frequently hear "My parents did not talk to me about what was going on", or "I couldn't talk to my parents because they don't listen, or are not interested in how I feel." Children need to know the truth of what is going on and understand that they will be looked after regardless.

Adrienne Rich wrote a book called *"On Lies, Secrets and Silence"*

(1966). I will quote some of the material from that book as the author has a different and perhaps better way of describing some of what I wanted to say in this chapter.

"Lying is done with words and also with silence."

Within relationships we often lie to others without being openly aware of it, because to tell the truth will cause us to confront our primal pain. In my younger does I used to lightly punch a female I liked on the shoulder. I was surprised when they resented this type of approach. Now I know it was much easier for me to punch someone lightly (avoiding my feelings) rather than tell them directly that I liked them a lot. Telling them directly would be the truth but that would also bring up my pain of not being loved as a child.

Rich writes *"The liar lives in fear of losing control. She cannot even desire a relationship without manipulation, since to be vulnerable to another person means for her the loss of control. The liar has many friends and leads an existence of great loneliness".*

"In lying to others we end up lying to ourselves." (to keep away from pain)

"The unconscious wants truth as the body does."

This last sentence by Rich is better understood from a primal perspective, and I mention it because it is almost impossible for a person who is undergoing primal therapy to stop the truth from emerging during therapy, as I mentioned earlier. The unconscious knows that pain attached to a traumatic memory is a toxic force and wants it out of the body. Facing the truth of that memory is the difficult part because it also unlocks the pain for us to feel.

Rich. *"We take so much of the universe on trust. I allow my universe to change in minute significant ways, on the basis of things you have said to me, of my trust in you. When we discover that someone we trusted can be trusted no longer, it forces us to question the whole instinct of trust."*

When a trust is broken it can blow a relationship apart, and Rich describes it like this, *"For a while, we are thrust back into some bleak, jutting edge, in a dark pierced by sheets of fire, swept by sheets of rain, in a world before kinship, a naming, or tenderness exist; we are brought close to formlessness."*

There are two things said by Rich that I will comment on. The first one is the mention of 'fire', which is also used by many people to describe aspects of love (see chapter on Nature of Love). Whether we feel good or bad, the sensations ultimately give us a 'burning' feeling, which reflects the intensity of the first level of consciousness that is ignited in close relationships.

The second comment is on the use of the word "formlessness". Love is the ultimate feeling and gives us a strong sense of self. When love is taken away we then feel an emptiness, or a sense of not knowing who we are, which can also be described as *formlessness*. These feelings are experienced by everybody who does primal therapy for long enough to get to the first level of consciousness. Not receiving a parent's love in childhood is a severe breach of trust and creates a human who is not whole, or feels they have no 'form'.

Truth and trust are needed if the most intimate of human relationships are to flourish.

On a larger scale there are nations who do not trust each other, and also governments that do not trust their populations with the freedoms that we all need as humans. Governments should not be trying to control their citizens by force. What they should be doing is introducing programmes that aim to raise every citizens Global Area of Love score to 80 or better. At this level of functioning people will be more willing to tell the truth, and have trust that others have their best interests at heart.

Unfortunately the need to block primal pain also blocks access to our loving and altruistic nature, and truth and trust become collateral damage in that process. As I discussed earlier in this chapter, truth and trust expressed within and between human social groups became an integral part of our evolutionary survival mechanism. Treating truth and trust lightly is part of our fatal flaw because removing them may leave us vulnerable to extinction.

RESEARCH

and the Three Levels of Consciousness

Modern day scientific research into the human condition is based mostly on the third level of consciousness. The research is formulated, conducted and analysed from the cognitive level of the mind. Undertaking any research into human behaviour without understanding and factoring in the forces of the lower brains will lead to almost meaningless results and incorrect interpretations. Much of the research uses patient self-report and this is obviously a third level cognitive view, which is usually highly distorted because of underlying primal pain.

Using the house analogy, modern day scientists and researchers will only understand the human condition if they leave their penthouse and go and explore the feeling rooms and then the basement of their minds. This learning is not available from a lecture or from personal deductions and theories. It is a 'felt' experience and so the person wishing to understand the brain at this level needs to go into a padded sound proof room where a trained therapist will guide them on their journey into sensations and feelings. If the patient has a lot of primal pain then they will need to be ready for an emotionally rough journey. From this perspective a new science of sensations and feelings needs to emerge, which will be radically different from the third level view of science that dominates at the moment.

Love itself is a pure sensation at the first level, and when primal pain distorts its journey upwards in the brain it becomes too much of a subjective experience at the third level for scientists and people in general to understand its nature.

Love may be more like gravity, where its forces cannot be seen, but its effects have scientific formulation, similar to gravity having a known rate of acceleration of a falling object and also its maximum velocity. The orbits of the moon around the earth and then the earth and other planets around the sun are governed by gravitational forces. These forces are so reliable that astronomers can predict planetary eclipses and ocean tides with incredible accuracy.

At the moment I believe we have enough research information to give a person a reasonably accurate GAL score, and that a GAL score, or similar mental health measure, will become a very important variable in future brain and social science research. Maybe when science starts to understand the power and nature of love they will be able to determine a GAL score with the same accuracy they have with gravity and astronomy.

There are already some scales being developed within the psych industry that could be part of determining a GAL score. The following is from a TED talk by Dr Nadine Burke. Kaiser Permanente developed a ten point Adverse Childhood Experience (ACE) questionnaire to determine a respondents' exposure to childhood trauma. The list contained psychological abuse, physical abuse, sexual abuse, substance abuse by a parent, domestic violence towards their mother, parent separation or divorce and parent mental illness. The higher the ACE score the more likely the person was to have a mental health issue. (The research also showed that high scores also predicted increased physical problems as well, which seemed to surprise them. Many people, especially those in alternative or natural medicine who are familiar with the disease process, have known for a very long time that psychological problems, sometimes referred to as a sick soul, will cause problems in the physical body. The present day drug dominated medical model of healing apparently does not contain any teaching about the importance of the relationship between psychological problems and physical disease).

Even though the ACE score only targets a small window in the overall view of mental health, it fits well within the proposed GAL score concept which provides for the bigger picture. The problem with the ACE research is that it is only dealing with one side of an equation, in that it is proving causes but not providing a cure. From reading on the internet I see that many therapists are rushing to use the common cognitive type therapies, such as meditation, positive thinking and even yoga to try and treat adverse childhood experiences (which all come about due to an unloving environment). These third level of mind therapies do not affect the first level where the real problem lays.

The social sciences are dominated by research and treatment in three main areas, those being genetics, medication and cognitive behaviour therapy. When these three treatment areas are contrasted with the three levels of consciousness therapy, it is easy to understand why their effect is very limited in overcoming the mental disorders of the human race.

Genetics

Twenty years ago, when I had my mental breakdown, it was widely thought that our genes control much of our lives. Therefore my depression, anxiety and addictions could somehow be put down to faulty genes inherited from my parents. Since then there has been a monumental shift and it is now known that the environment can alter our gene expression, not so much for physical things like hair colour and body shape, but for psychological attributes that define our personalities, as well as susceptibility to mental disorders.

The study of methylation and other chemical processes in the human genome (epigenetics) is showing that traumatised babies and children are the ones at most risk of developing a mental disorder, and that mental disorders are the result of these gene variants. From the University of Wisconson, Madison. *'Nearly one million children in the United States are neglected or abused each year. Maltreated children had extra methylation on certain genes. This malformation was related to the risk of developing mental and physical problems'*.

Despite this research and many other similar studies there is not total agreement among researchers that early environment causes the gene variation. This type of research is a good example of having lots of data but no over-arching paradigm in which to fit it. Therefore researchers can put a lot of 'dots' on a map of mental health but no-one seems to be connecting these dots. For example despite all the research showing that trauma in childhood causes almost all mental illness, there are many professionals who still believe that depression and anxiety are primarily caused by chemical imbalances in the brain, while others are pursuing genetic causes.

Because I understand primal theory and have undergone primal therapy, I can interpret any research in those terms, which allows me to join many of the 'dots'. Now I feel confident in making the bold statement that almost all mental health disorders result from lack of love in childhood. I can't recall ever reading about any research that would dispute my statement. In fact the current research into epigenetics is strongly supportive of the above statement. If we want to stop the increase in mental disorders we need to confront this truth head on.

Not all the trauma that causes mental disorders occurs in childhood. Things like Post Traumatic Stress Disorder (PTSD) can develop in adults but the root cause is still lack of love. For example battlefields produce soldiers who suffer from PTSD, but there is very little love on a battlefield. Seeing people being blown apart and fearing their own death produces a traumatic stress reaction in the individuals psyche. No amount of mind control during training can overcome that effect.

If it is the early unloving environment that has caused the methylation, wouldn't it make sense to reverse the situation? Early intervention type therapies do this to some degree, in that they try to convert the home environment into a more loving one. This helps to limit the damage but does not reverse that already done; not to a large degree anyway. Primal pain causes methylation, so releasing that pain, as primal therapy does, may be the only way to reverse the methylation. Future research that includes an understanding of the three levels of consciousness and the nature of love will determine all the above issues.

In my own case I had suicidal depression, anxiety and several addictions. After undergoing primal therapy there is no doubt in my mind that my suffering was caused by lack of love early in life, and not by faulty genes. The amount of primal pain I have released is phenomenal, and I am still amazed how that much pain could be stored in my body without my being aware of it. I now see my childhood trauma as being a type of PTSD. I am sure methylation and other epigenetic activity is involved and science will eventually be able to explain how it all happens. The good thing is that the effects of my traumatic past have been reversed. This knowledge is important because there are still many professionals who believe traumatic imprinting is irreversible, and others who say the past is too dark to deal with.

In any case the study of genetics will always be incomplete without the understanding of the effects of love or no love at the first level of consciousness to influence epigenetic structure and expression.

Medication

There is a widespread belief in the medical community that many mental health problems are caused by an imbalance of chemicals in the brain. The most common treatment for depression and anxiety is medication that increases the amount of serotonin in the brain, which reduces symptoms. By the medical professions own admission they do not understand how this happens. Primal theory says the terror imprinted in the brainstem is always trying to force its way into the second and third levels of consciousness. Serotonin is a pain signal modifier, in that it lets us feel some pain, but not enough to overwhelm the third level. When we take an SSRI we are blocking most of the psychological pain signals between the first and third levels. In this way sheer terror in the brainstem is modified down to some level of anxiety in the prefrontal cortex.

In shutting down the lines of connection any good feelings are also blocked. That is why people on SSRI medication report not being able to feel much at all. When the medication is stopped the serotonin levels drop and the pain signals get through again, which means a return of symptoms. The underlying cause at the first level has not been touched. I believe it is this level that causes the chemical imbalances in the upper parts of the brain in the first place.

Research shows medication has the ability to reduce symptoms of disorders like depression and anxiety. But not having a baseline of what good mental health is, such as a GAL score would provide, means not having any idea of where to fit research results, or how effective any given therapy is. For example, with my GAL score of 50 I suffered depression, the medical profession gave me an SSRI, and I felt better in the sense I ceased to feel much at all. So this is seen as a good outcome for medication. But it did not raise my GAL score, and I had no idea that much better was possible. I remained oblivious to the fact that there was a much better way of being in this world other than having a GAL score of 50 and taking medication.

Undergoing primal therapy raised my GAL score to 85 and this is a much better way of experiencing my life. Medication turned me into an unfeeling robot and primal therapy returned feeling to my body.

Notwithstanding all the research results showing that an unloved childhood causes mental illness, there is still a lot of emphasis being placed on the genetic and medication pathway to cure.

The 'Psychiatric Genetics' journal published the following,

Genetic Trigger for Schizophrenia and Alcoholism Discovered.

'People who have a rare variant of the GRM3 gene are two to three times more likely to develop schizophrenia, alcoholism and bi-polar disorder than people with the more common expression of the gene. Psychiatrist Professor David Curtis led the study that looked at the genes of 4,971 people who had been diagnosed with schizophrenia, bi-polar and alcoholism, and compared their genes to 1,309 healthy people.'

'They found those with a mental illness were much more likely to have the rare gene variant, and now they are hopeful the finding will

pave the way for new psychiatric drugs.'

"We could be looking at the next big drug target for treating mental illness," Professor Curtis said.

I am not a scientist or statistician, but there are a few things I wish to comment on in this study. How many of the 4,971 people with a mental disorder had traumatic childhoods, and how many of 1,309 had loving parents? This is an example of a study where a GAL score would provide a very important variable, and without it the results have much less meaning. From a primal theory viewpoint I would hypothesise that the 4,971 with a mental disorder would have a much lower average GAL score than the control group.

There is a lot of research happening that shows an unloved childhood produces mentally disturbed children and adults, and yet this knowledge is not part of this study. This is a common theme for a lot of research at the present because it is all done on an individual or 'very small view' basis, that has no over-riding paradigm in which to conduct the research and analyse the results. Including a GAL score and analysing the results under the umbrella that primal theory provides would make the above research much more meaningful.

"We could be looking at the next big drug target for treating mental illness" the professor said.

This is becoming a very common statement in genetic research. I assume they mean a drug that targets the gene variants, and by altering the variant it will cure mental disorders. I am not sure this technology even exists at the moment, and it may not be possible anyway.

Consider this point if you will. Undergoing primal therapy informs the person that their mental illness, whatever it is, is caused by a lack of love in the earliest years of life. Suppose scientists develop a drug that cures mental illness. Does that mean we will be able to ignore, bash and sexually abuse our children, and when they develop a mental disorder we can give them a drug that turns them into loving, well-behaved adults that are thrilled to be alive?

The point I am trying to make is that a lot of research is proving useless in understanding the human condition, because it does not understand the three levels of consciousness. Looking for drugs to fix third level symptoms will surely prove futile, because the strength and power to change gene expression lies at the first level. Our lower brain has the power to change gene expression in response to the environment it finds itself in, and it does so through gene variants. The imbalance of chemicals in the brain is caused by gene variants.

Chemicals in the form of neurotransmitters or hormones are only the messengers, they are not the original authors.

Cognitive behavioural type therapies

Cognitive behavioural type therapies are also known as 'talk' therapies, and consist of a narrative between therapist and patient. Lious Cozolino in *The Neuroscience of Psychotherapy,* second edition, page 163. *While psychotherapy is a relatively recent and culture specific development in human history, talking to one another, seeking out advice, and exchanging stories likely go back to the first humans. Thus the talking cure exists within a matrix of beings who share the gift of the gab. I suggest to you that the evolution of the brain and the development of narratives have gone hand in hand.*

Well yes, I agree, to a point. Narrative would be involved in the development of the human brain, but only in recent history. Remember that the human species started off as a type of sea slug on the ocean floor. Over millions of years we first developed a sensing brain that we now refer to as the reptilian brain, and in the human brain this is our brainstem. It is what this book refers to as the third level of consciousness. This means we went through a stage in our evolution when we were capable of surviving on our senses alone.

The next part of the brain to evolve was the limbic system, which gave us the ability to feel – the second level of consciousness. So we also went through an evolutionary period where we survived quite well on sensations and feelings. That means that we communicated through our senses and feelings only. Much of our communication is still done this way, only we generally do not recognise what's happening in our lower brains because primal pain and repression are blocking access to these levels. When the sensations and feelings do get through we do not recognise them for what they are (see chapter on altered mind states). Sensations and feelings are also the dominant communication tool used by infants up to about 18 months of age, and only then is the narrative added. Successful communication between a baby and adult relies on sensations and feelings, also described as intuition or gut feeling - provided they are generated by an un-traumatised brainstem.

The cortex developed later and gave us our thinking ability, and then speech (narrative) to express our thoughts. This is the third level of consciousness. The hearing centre (Broca's Area) and speech formation centre (Wernicke's Area) are both situated in the cortex. So our senses came first and predate the narrative part of our brains, perhaps by millions of years.

It is obvious Cozolino and many other researchers in this day and age do not understand the brain from the perspective of evolution and the three levels of consciousness, and therefore do not understand that narrative has very little effect on the sensing brain. It is pointless trying to persuade the first level to behave itself by talking to it, because it does not understand speech. Our powerful senses drive what we feel, and feelings then drive what we think and believe. That was and is the progression in evolution.

Any therapy at all that requires mental gymnastics from the thinking mind is doomed to failure. As an example meditation and/or mindfulness is becoming very popular in all healing modalities, from both the medical and complementary viewpoints. Scientists at UCLA have found a relationship between the length of time a person has been meditating to the thickening of areas within the cortex. And Cozolino again on page 254 *"and when we successfully use cognitive techniques to decrease anxiety, we are likely building these descending cortical networks to inhibit amygdale and autonomic activation"*.

So what is really happening here? Primal theory would say the thickening of the cortical areas is due to the meditation blocking out pain signals from below, and constant practise thickens up these areas. The person then feels better because the pain signals are blocked by a densely packed pathway. This is a similar action to medication, in that it reduces the connection between levels. I am familiar with the effects of meditation on a personal level because I studied and practised under an Indian Guru for twelve months.

In contrast the aim of primal therapy is to open up these pathways to access the primal pain being held on the first level. As primal pain is released these same pathways allow love to flow freely; it is no longer repressed – access to love is no longer denied. During primal therapy any form of mind control such as meditation and mindfulness is not allowed, because it helps to block access to the lower levels. (Mindfulness type therapies are rampant at the moment and this is anathema to a person versed in primal therapy because we understand it actually deals with unfavourable emotions by blocking *all* feeling, including love).

The following is taken from an article on the web on meditation *'However, to maintain your gains you have to keep meditating. Why? Because the brain can very easily revert back to its old ways if you are not vigilant. This means you have to keep meditating to ensure that the new neural pathways you worked so hard to form stay strong.*

In primal therapy terms we want the gates of communication to open up, as a contrast to so many other commonly used therapies that close the gates tighter on any feelings.

As an example I recently went on a coffee date. The lady had worked in a child protection agency and seemed to know all about unresolved primal pain, and the damage that parents can do when they don't apply true love to parenting. The way she dealt with her own uncomfortable emotions was to sit quietly and tap herself in a particular spot, such as the head, chest or arm until the feeling went away. At this moment I knew that a deep relationship with this person was not possible, because 'tapping' represses feelings, and love is a feeling. A person cannot choose to repress bad feelings and then express the good ones – the brain does not work that way.

Of more concern to myself is what is happening in our schools to deal with the ever-increasing uncontrollable emotions that children are displaying. The teachers are instructing the affected children to sit quietly and breathe deeply until the emotion subsides. Many newspaper articles are lauding the results of this approach, but to a primal person it borders on horrific, because although immediate results can be impressive, what is actually happening is suppression of feeling. Teaching a child how not to feel will have disastrous results in the long term for themselves and those they are supposed to love.

Narrative is still important in human lives, and if we have full connection on all three levels, our implicit moral system means we will talk sense (from our pure uncluttered sense of love). Being blocked between levels leads to our talk being influenced by our defence system, which means our narrative is being censored to keep our pain at bay, so we end up talking no sense, which we call nonsense. We all know that many belief systems are just nonsense, but the owner needs his belief system to keep his primal pain repressed.

In a lot of cases the current human narrative has become almost useless, in fact very detrimental, because we cannot have truth and trust in something that is formed and driven by the need to repress primal pain. And we certainly can't trust it as a healing tool. For example young children are introduced to religion by a narrative that is mostly driven by a dogmatic belief system. A significant amount of people who seek healing from psychological problems, have those problems because of religious indoctrination. To develop in a healthy way children need a narrative that is generated from pure love, and when they have that they don't need religion. As I have tried to explain pure love is the ultimate experience of mankind. Religion tries to emulate the ideals of pure love, but it becomes hijacked by the fatal flaw in the human brain.

If we accept the fact that for true healing we need a therapy that removes primal pain, then it becomes important for individuals to choose a therapy which uses feelings that will ultimately release primal pain at the first level, rather than one which uses a narrative for healing, which can only ever partly address the third level.

There are many new types of therapies available, and one of them is called Acceptance and Commitment Therapy. The acceptance part accepts the fact that one's life was not ideal, and unfavourable emotions generally ruled. The commitment part was to move forward regardless. A reviewer of the book wrote *"This approach helps you move forward with your life regardless of whether you are 'better' or not. It helps you get on with your life despite your illness. The therapy helps in anxiety, depression and PTSD etc."* This therapy is using the cognitive brain to work out and then force a solution, and although it is said to be a new and innovative therapy, it is really just a re-hash of positive thinking, which suppresses feeling while trying to strengthen the narrative. The examples I gave above of the 'tapping' lady and the 'sit quietly' school children are both examples of using the cognitive brain when the problem is with the first level sensations. Another quote from David Bohm, *"If you engage in positive thinking to overcome negative thoughts, the negative thoughts are still there acting. That's still incoherence. It's not enough just to engage in positive thoughts when you have negative thoughts registered, because they keep on working and will cause trouble somewhere else."*

As a contrast primal therapy understands the importance of underlying feeling, and a therapy session takes place in a padded soundproof room where those feelings are encouraged to come forth and be processed. Very little narrative and/or cognition is used. The cause of the unfavourable emotions is explained within the underlying feelings and sensations, which are the languages of the lower brain that most humans do not understand.

Professional doubts

Most of the psych profession adhere stoically to the fact that their treatments are based on empirical evidence-based research, although this evidence only considers one level of human functioning when there are in fact three levels. Not surprisingly everybody is not happy with the outcomes this has produced. Cozolino (p 357) *"It is humbling and more than a little frightening to realize that we rely on what may be the* most complex structure in the Universe with little knowledge of how it works."

Dr Joseph Glenmuller, a Harvard Medical School Professor. "*While there has been no shortage of alleged biochemical explanations for psychiatric conditions ... not one has been proven. Quite the contrary. In every instance where such an imbalance was thought to have been found it was later proven false.*"

Dr David Kaiser, Psychiatrist. *Psychiatry makes unproven claims that depression, bipolar illness, anxiety, alcoholism and a host of other disorders are in fact biologic and probably genetic in origin. This kind of faith in science and progress is staggering, not to mention naive and perhaps delusional.*

Thomas Insell. Director of the American National Institute of Mental Health, blogging about the death of Robin Williams, a well known movie star. "*We in the mental health community speak a lot about recovery, but the inconvenient truth is that for too many people, mental illness can be fatal. While shame or prejudice, lack of access, or poor quality care can all contribute to fatal outcomes, even those who have had access to the best available care still, too often, die from depression.*" And elsewhere, "*For mental disorders we do not know the cause, we lack a biomarker that is 100% accurate for diagnosis, and there is no treatment programme equivalent to ART for HIV.*" (treatment for Aids).

James W Prescott, psychiatrist, (from his website). '*We have culturally evolved a deranged brain of modern homo sapiens that defies all therapies and interventions for change. Our neocortical brain has corrupted our sub-cortical limbic, sexual, emotional and social brain, which holds little promise of transformation.*"

Thomas Insell again. "*Advances in systems neuroscience, from dissecting circuits to human brain imaging, are unequivocally stunning. But, and this is a humbling caveat, we simply have not been able to translate this revolution in neuroscience to diagnostic or therapeutics for people with mental disorders.*"

Steve Diamond. (I used this quote earlier in the book but it is also very relevant for this section. "*If psychotherapy as a healing of the soul (not just the mind) is to survive and thrive in the future, our recent over-emphasis on cognition, behaviour, genetics, neurology and biochemistry must be counterbalanced by the inclusion of the spiritual and depth psychological dimensions of human existence.*"

Understanding the human brain from the perspective of its three levels of consciousness, with the first level being the dominant level, and not the third, would solve most of the above mentioned problems.

What they are doing about the crisis in mental health?

There are many separate faculties within universities that study the human condition. This approach does not seem to be solving problems on a large scale, so the trend now is to set up organisations that bring all the disparate information together and try and make something meaningful out of that. I guess in some way they are trying to join the dots.

UNI LAUNCHES BRAVE BID TO CURE HUMANITY *(headline)*

Professor Stephen Simpson of the University of Sydney is in charge of a $500 million attempt to save humanity from itself. The article says thousand's of academics across all sixteen University faculties will share their knowledge. Their task is to find solutions for obesity, diabetes and cardiovascular disease.

The Roston and Harvard Universities in America are taking the same approach. Also in America they are throwing mega-dollars at the problem. Thomas Insell once more on June 11th 2014. *"We know much less about the brain than any other organ, and yet brain disorders, from autism to Alzheimers, are increasing in prevalence, creating a national public health crisis. Recognising both the urgency and the complexity, the Brain Report calls for a broad approach, involving $4.5 billion investment over 10 years to decode the language of the brain by understanding its circuits."* He also adds *"Freeman Dyson, a leading astrophysicist, famously said 'New directions in science are launched by new tools much more often than by new concepts.' This is true for neuroscience as much as astrophysics. The Rosetta Stone for the brain will require a new generation of tools that give us the vocabulary, the syntax and the grammar of the brain."*

My comments on the above.

1. The vocabulary, syntax and grammar of the brain has more to do with sensations and feelings rather than circuits. Tracing the circuits will only show where the signals flow, not what they are 'saying'. For that understanding a person needs to lay down in a padded room and become overwhelmed with sensation and feelings – only then will he or she be able to understand the language of the brain.

2. New tools may help, but in my opinion we already have enough technology. What we need are new ways to interpret the knowledge we already have. Primal therapy is simplistic in that it has

padded rooms and nothing much more is required. I cured my depression and anxiety by releasing my primal pain in a padded room. Neither my therapist nor myself needed to know anything at all about the physical aspects of the brain for treatment to be successful. Studying the brain and its workings may be a fascinating pastime, but it is not necessary in finding causes and cures for mental health. We have already manifested that knowledge on this earth in the form of Janovian Primal Theory and Therapy. This knowledge is proving hard to disseminate because it is not intellectual in nature.

3. New tools like the microscope and telescope have certainly helped science, but what is needed in mental health are not new tools, as Freeman Dyson suggests above, but a new concept. Combining departments and sharing information is really just going down the same old path. If you combine twenty intellectually based departments, you are going to get an intellectually based answer. The three levels of consciousness, with the power of love coming from the first level, will provide the totally new concept that is needed.

APPENDIX

Global Area Of Love (GAL) Score

90 – 100

Supreme functioning, life dominated by feelings of love

Monogamous heterosexual.

Had loving parents

Only eats healthy food and drinks, looks after self and others.

Has many good friends and strong relationships.

No depression, anxiety, addictions or irrational beliefs.

Stays healthy and disease free into old age.

Truthful and trustful. Very happy.

Many bio-markers of good health, eg low cortisol, no inflammatory processes in body, high oxytocins, very little methylation of DNA, normal blood pressure.

Good neuronal activity e.g. heart rhythms, sleep patterns, brain activity.

80 – 90

Very good relationships, life runs smoothly.

Happy to be alive

Good diet, exercises regularly

Minor symptoms of anxiety, depression and anger, but of low intensity and transient in nature.

No smoking, no recreational drugs, minimum alcohol.

70 – 80

80 is the level of feeling required for an adequate flow of oxytocins, and

all the healthy benefits that accrue from that level. When a GAL score falls below 80 life itself becomes more and more of a struggle, with mental and physical disorders becoming increasingly intense.

Minor relationship problems, some social problems.

No smoking, moderate alcohol, becoming careless about good diet.

Some anxiety and low moods but easily controlled.

Start to question the meaning of life.

Not so happy

60 – 70

Relationship problems, divorce a possibility.

Sexual problems such as painful sex and frigidity.

Social problems affect quality of life, becoming self centred.

Poor food choices, abusing alcohol, smoking.

Depressive episodes and anxiety becoming more frequent and intense.

Bio – markers and neuronal activity falling away from normal, or what is possible under ideal conditions.

Maybe had two parents that tolerate each other for a convenient life, but no real love between them

50 – 60

No long lasting relationships, divorce very likely, major social problems.

Sexual problems increase, reliance on comfort foods.

Substance abuse, heavy smoker, physical sickness.

Cares less about personal appearance, or becomes obsessive/compulsive.

Severe depression, anxiety and addictions.

Unhappy, lots of sadness in life

Irrational beliefs to help hold primal pain at bay.

Truth and trust are abused. Very neurotic.

Single parent or two parents who squabble frequently and/ or ignore the child.

40 – 50

At a level of 50 the person is very neurotic, and below this becomes increasingly psychotic.

No long lasting close relationships, antisocial behaviour.

Difficulty in orgasm. Frigidity or compulsive sex.

Abuses alcohol, smokes heavily, drug use out of control.

Anorexia, anger, severe anxiety and depression.

Addictions ruin life, irrational, extreme narcissism.

Suicidal thoughts. Harming others.

Bio-markers and neuronal activity at extreme plus or minus levels.

Brain scans show abnormalities in brain areas, such as volumes and 'tangles'.

30 – 40

Very antisocial, life has no meaning or joy.

Harms self and others, suicidal.

Does not look after self. Poor food choices.

Irrational, insanity, loosing touch with reality.

Very angry, severely depressed.

30 and below

Insanity.

Personal hygiene problems.

Violent. Will kill self or others.

H southgrp

JCPG2E   3B

J7QLFG   2

                    3A -
                              3

18 —

31F

Made in the USA
San Bernardino, CA
04 January 2018